DORSET~AMERICA

DORSET~AMERICA

THE STORY OF DORSET'S LINKS WITH
NORTH AMERICA THROUGH THE CENTURIES

RODNEY LEGG

DORSET BOOKS

First published in Great Britain in 2006

British Library Cataloguing-in-Publication Data
A CIP record for this title is available from the British Library

ISBN 1 871164 47 8
ISBN 978 1 871164 47 3

DORSET BOOKS
Dorset Books is a partnership between
Dorset County Council and Halsgrove

Halsgrove House
Lower Moor Way
Tiverton, Devon EX16 6SS
Tel: 01884 243242
Fax: 01884 243325
email: sales@halsgrove.com
website: www.halsgrove.com

Printed and bound by CPI Bath Press, Bath.

DEDICATION
For Sandra and Tony Goddard
to take with them to the States.

CONTENTS

INTRODUCTION

The nineteenth century was the British century. The twentieth century was the American century. From clashes through to collusion the two nations and a dominion remain linked by common roots and what has become the world language. All British counties, each state of the Union, and every Canadian province have intimate links. These were highlighted by the Prince of Wales on his visit the United States in November 2005, when he called them 'the closest connections shared by any two nations in the world'. For reasons geographical, military and political, Dorset can claim as many as anywhere. Bonds of blood and culture stretch in both directions.

Transatlantic Dorset is the subject of this book.

Poole fishermen worked the Grand Banks off Newfoundland. Sir Walter Raleigh organised Sir Richard Grenville's ill-fated settlement of Roanoke Island, North Carolina, in 1585. He introduced tobacco to England and Sherborne. What smoking contributed to social pleasure, was equalled by the introduction of potatoes to the British diet, with both being consumed to excess. The first crops of potatoes from Virginia were grown around Bradford Abbas and stored in 'Tiddy Caves' at Nether Compton.

Lyme Regis seamen founded the mid-Atlantic colony of Bermuda after being shipwrecked there in 1609. The *Mayflower* passed by the Dorset cliffs on 15 August 1620 – next stop Plymouth – after setting off from the West Quay at Southampton. Dorchester pioneers and Weymouth mariners founded Massachusetts. The stars and stripes of 'Old Glory' can be seen on carvings at Affpuddle and Steeple, being the arms of Washington family ancestors who married into Dorset's Lawrence family.

In reverse, there were 'arms across the sea' – actual, material and metaphorical – through the great conflicts of the last century. The presence reached its climax in 1944 when Weymouth and Portland were pivotal in the storming of Omaha Beach in the biggest and bloodiest of the Normandy landings. Some 100,000 American troops, airmen and sailors were stationed in Dorset at the time. Of the greatest army ever based in Dorset, 5000 United States servicemen who passed through the county lost their lives in Europe. GI, incidentally, stood for General Issue, which was stencilled onto soldiers' kit.

It still raises eyebrows to say so, but these GIs came to win the war, at a time when the European powers had fought themselves to a standstill. Men and munitions began flowing across the Atlantic. Flying-boats from Poole, operated by British Overseas Airways Corporation, maintained VIP transatlantic services. Much American military hardware survives on display in the Tank Museum at Bovington Camp and in the Royal Signals Museum at Blandford.

Many Dorset families have intimate links with Canada and the United States. The Ismays from Iwerne Minister operated the White Star Fleet which we remember for *Titanic*. American ambassador Robert Worth Bingham boasted on arrival in London that he was 'one of the Binghams of Bingham's Melcombe, an old Dorsetshire family'. Both the Guest and Digby families married into the Spencer Churchill dynasty. Pamela Digby progressed to a second marriage with Leland Hayward and a third to

American diplomat Averell Harriman. She returned to Europe as United States Ambassador to Paris.

There are also numerous literary connections, from the States in the shape of John Lothrop Motley who died while visiting Dorset in 1877, to the Powys family of authors and lecturers who were in almost perpetual motion across the Atlantic. 'American admirers,' as they described themselves, were the first to erect a monument in England to novelist and poet Thomas Hardy. Thomas Hollis from Corscombe did it in reverse, with enormous

enthusiasm for all things libertarian and American, and proved it by creating the famous Harvard Library.

This book is a celebration of such associations and shrines for our American cousins. Few, however, are generally known on this side of the Atlantic. Finding them on the ground has been a process of discovering our own country. I have set out the results as an alphabetical gazetteer of the places concerned, listed chronologically in some cases, where there are multiple entries. Ordnance Survey map references are given to the locations.

Thomas Hollis of Corscombe, the rich book editor who endowed Harvard University Library, named fields and farms in Dorset for American associations.

ABBOTSBURY

John Cowper Powys

Abbotsbury Beach — SY 559 847

The author John Cowper Powys (1872–1964) spent much of his life lecturing in the United States. Though from Welsh roots his father was a West Country parson, initially as a curate in Dorchester, and then vicar of Montacute, Somerset, from 1886 to 1918. John was sent to Sherborne School. There the surrounding countryside provided the setting for the novel which by the close of the 1920s had sealed his literary reputation.

Powys Major, as he was known at school to distinguish him from younger brothers, roamed westwards from the ancient abbey town, across the long pasture of Lenthay Common and its former pond, to Bradford Abbas. The provincial centres of Yeovil, Dorchester and Weymouth — linked by a branch of the Great Western Railway — were 'the cities of my world'. The result, in 1929, was *Wolf Solent* and its reviewer for the *Sunday Times* was duly impressed:

'Its background is Dorset, and it is a Dorset which has rarely been painted more graciously, even by Hardy himself.'

The next major work from John Cowper Powys, *Weymouth Sands* in 1934, included a shipwreck scene set on the Chesil Beach at Abbotsbury. This spot stayed in Powys's mind and he asked for his ashes to be cast there. Once again, the novel won considerable acclaim, with Angus Wilson considering that he wrote 'not of heroes or even of men, but of men beside nature'.

Among his other novels are *Wood and Stone* and the period-piece *The Brazen Head*. Poetry included *Wolfsbane, Mandragora* and *Samphire*, and deeper thinking in *The Religion of a Sceptic* and *In Defence of Sensuality*. Literary criticism included *Visions and Revisions* and the *Meaning of Culture*, his *Autobiography, Morwyn* and *The Pleasures of Literature*.

Of the 48 United States — those of the pre-Hawaii and Alaska boundaries — John Cowper Powys missed only two. By his own account, he made some fifty crossings of the Atlantic, 'for I used at first to go home twice a year'. The first was on the old Cunarder *Ivernia* which was later sunk during the Second World War. On board he met G. Arnold Shaw and began a lastingly influential business friendship.

Shaw became 'the most perfect stage-manager' for the Powys lecture circuit. 'Put it all on me, John,' Shaw would say when Powys experienced one of his recurrent panic attacks. These tours went on for twenty-five years. Powys worked himself up into 'ecstasies of anger' with 'outbursts of intoxicated malice and infernal spleen'. He could drift into 'a hypnotism of speech' on subjects such as 'The Republic of the Future'.

This was seen from the perspective of a hedonistic philosophy — a stroke more avant-garde than that of fellow authors among his brothers. First, however, he reassured audiences that they were going to have their eclectic mix of philosophy and literary appreciation approached from the safer ground of sympathetic xenophobia:

'I love America. Even the Russians love America. We delight in the beauty of the paradox because you have not found social democracy but you are the most perfect bourgeois proletarians. Bravado and boasting are in your nature but they are not allowed to invade your souls. You are authentic people and to me the United States is a true democracy. Here I come to escape from pompous English humbug.'

Such displays of intellectual emotion went down well with audiences who shared dogmatic if divergent opinions. He reflected that 'those who liked me best were

Jews, Communists and Catholics'. His young American friend and poet Arthur Davison Ficke (1883–1945) captured the unique experience of a Powys lecture in verse. Powys, in his turn, became the protégé of Charles Erskine Scott Wood, 'that noble old Poseidon of the Pacific'.

RMS *Mauretania* was John Cowper Powys's favourite liner and he described how she used to 'cut the water like a horizontal guillotine'. This vessel returns to our story in the entry for Hamworthy. Powys devotees who know their subject have made the pilgrimage to visit its stylish remains in Lake Drive. This is where author and ocean come together. The passage of time adds value to the potency of such relics. The sea flowed through the author's life and it was therefore appropriate that the self-styled 're-incarnation of Taliessin' was laid to rest neither in Shirley in Derbyshire where he was born or the Land of his Fathers where he died on

17 June 1963. (His wife, Margaret Alice Lyon, predeceased him in 1947.)

The ashes of the great spirit of ancient Welsh Druidism were cast on the sea, as Powys wished, at the point where Dorset faces the great ocean where he had sailed so many times. The chosen spot, into the swell of Lyme Bay, was from the shingle on the western side of the great Chesil Beach, just beyond the seaward end of the road that passes the Sub Tropical Gardens at Abbotsbury.

Powys was survived by his dedicated American admirer, Miss Phyllis Playter, who had been his companion for more than four decades. The couple maintained their transatlantic connections. In particular, until his death in 1962, they continued to hear from Edwin Estlin Cummings – the American poet e. e. cummings – who had been their neighbour at Patchin Place in Greenwich Village.

State-side lecturer and author John Cowper Powys, as painted by his sister, Gertrude Powys.

AFFPUDDLE

George Washington

Affpuddle parish church — SY 805 937

The coat of arms on the north wall of the chancel is identical with that on the signet ring of George Washington (1732–99), the first President of the United States. The stars and stripes (or bars and mullets, to use the correct heraldic term) of the Washington family joined the Crusader cross of the Lawrences with the marriage of Edmund Lawrence and Agnes de Wessington, in 1390.

They appear on the elegant scrolled red-painted wall-monument to Edward Lawrence, who died in 1751.

More examples decorate Steeple Church in the Isle of Purbeck.

The Lawrence-Washington family arms of stars and stripes adorn the memorial to Edward Lawrence (1684–1751) in Affpuddle parish church.

BEAMINSTER

Samuel Hearne

Beaminster town — ST 480 013

The Canadian explorer Samuel Hearne (1745–92) lived as a youth in Beaminster. Many there recalled him in 1770 when news came back to Britain that he had spent three years in finding the passage through the icy waters along the north-western edge of America. Businessmen, geographers and mariners had come together, over-optimistically, to search for what was thought to be an arctic route into the Pacific.

Samuel Hearne went to sea as a youth. After having served as a midshipman under Captain Samuel Hood, he left the Royal Navy for the Hudson's Bay Company, in 1768. Following three attempts at forcing the North West Passage he then set off on foot, in 1771, along the Coppermine River and continued southwards across country for 1300 miles, until he reached the Great Slave Lake.

It shows the then current lack of knowledge about the shape of the North American continent that he could think he had reached 'Hyperborean Sea' which was thought to lie on the north-west coast of North America. On returning with this exciting news to Prince of Wales's Fort, on 30 June 1772, he instantly achieved heroic status. His career flourished and he established Fort Cumberland on his next expedition, in 1774, and was then appointed Governor of Prince of Wales's Fort.

In 1782, Samuel Hearne was taken prisoner on its capture by the French naval commander, Comte de La Perousem, and returned to England in 1787. By this time it was becoming obvious that he had failed to find an effective short cut between the world's two great oceans. Hearne died in 1792 and the book of his supposedly momentous trek, *An Account of the Journey from Hudson's Bay to the Northern Ocean*, was published posthumously in 1795.

BINGHAM'S MELCOMBE

Robert Worth Bingham

Bingham's Melcombe House — ST 772 021

In the heart of the county, towards the northern edge of the Dorset Downs between Cheselbourne and Ansty, this was the ancestral home of Robert Worth Bingham (1871–1937). The American newspaper publisher and diplomat always talked of his British roots and was sent home on behalf of his country, as United States Ambassador to London during the gathering storm that was the prelude to the Second World War, from 1933 until his untimely death in 1937.

He brought up his origins on the occasion of every suitable introduction, including each of his accreditations at the Court of St James, with the three Kings of those troubled years. King George V, who died after his Silver Jubilee celebrations, was briefly replaced by King Edward VIII until the Abdication, and then by the Duke of York as King George VI. Robert Worth Bingham always went straight to the point:

'I'm proud to be a Bingham of Bingham's Melcombe, in the most beautiful part of your country that's known as Dorset.'

Bingham's Melcombe House.

Back across the pond, he had been the owner of the Louisville *Courier-Journal* and the Louisville *Times*. Bingham was among the first in Europe to know the secrets of the love affair of the century between Edward and Mrs Simpson before the *New York Journal* made its sensational prediction 'King Will Wed Wally' and stated that, after the Coronation, the as yet not divorced Mrs Wallis Simpson would become the King's consort. The newspaper report read:

'King Edward believes that the most important thing for the peace and welfare of the world is an intimate understanding and relationship between England and America and that his marriage with this very gifted lady may help to bring about that beneficial co-operation between English speaking nations.'

Some sensed otherwise. Through his wife, Bingham's colleague and counterpart in Oslo, wealthy Anthony J. Drexel Biddle Jnr from Philadelphia who was Minister to Norway, placed a substantial winning bet that the King would abdicate.

Bingham family arms as the centrepiece to historic Bingham's Melcombe House.

Bingham's Melcombe can claim the oldest and largest yew hedge in Britain and Europe.

BLANDFORD

American General Hospital

Blandford Camp – ST 912 075

Roosevelt Park memorial garden commemorates the wartime use of Blandford Camp by the 22nd General Hospital of the United States Army. It was established in April 1944 in the Benbow Lines at Blandford Camp and then extended after the Battle of Normandy into a much bigger complex around the Anson-Craddock Lines. These are remembered for their connections with Great War poet Rupert Brooke, and artist and calligrapher Eric Gill, of the Royal Naval Division which trained here for the Gallipoli landings in the Dardanelles.

Blandford also provided Hospital Base Headquarters for American administrative and medical staff of the 119th, 125th, 131st and 140th General Hospitals. In 1944 the biggest influx of casualties came after the Battle of the Bulge, at Christmas, following the final German counter-offensive of the war through the snowy forests of the Ardennes. Arrivals, as many as 500 on just one night, were ferried into Dorset by a fleet of C-47 Dakota transports. Most were landed at RAF Tarrant Rushton.

The American occupation of Dorset's garrison town is marked by exhibits in the Royal Signals Museum which is open to members of the public provided they obtain security clearance at the main gate in Black Lane.

Dedication of Roosevelt Park and its memorial was carried out by Colonel Daniel J. Fourrier and Colonel Leonard D. Heaton – newly transferred from Pearl Harbor – on 30 May 1945. It was the first overseas plot to be named in tribute to the late President, Franklin Delano Roosevelt, who died as the European war came to a close.

Wartime President Franklin D. Roosevelt whose first overseas memorial was a commemorative garden at Blandford Camp.

The garden has since been re-titled the Roosevelt Memorial Garden and Monument with its 6-feet high stone having been the focus for United States Honor and Color Guards marching to 'The Stars and Stripes Forever' at a succession of 4th July celebrations. Plants in the garden are the descendants of seeds and saplings sent to Blandford from a total of 22 different States. Much of the original work was carried out by Private George H. Stuber of Yonkers, New York, as the active part of his convalescence.

Men of the 22nd General Hospital of United States Army, at Blandford Camp, paying tribute to their late President on 30 May 1945.

BLANDFORD

Royal Signals Museum

also at Blandford Camp

Several items of ground-breaking American radio technology from the Second World War have their place in the display cases of the Royal Signals Museum at Blandford Camp. This is open to members of the public, including overseas visitors, provided they obtain security clearance at the main gate in Black Lane.

The largest of the American exhibits is a huge valve, taller than a person, which belonged to the black propaganda project codenamed Aspidistra. This broadcast clandestine disinformation and misinformation on German wavelengths to cause confusion and demoralisation. Valve GL 898A, manufactured by General Electric, was installed at King's Standing, near Crowborough, in Ashdown Forest, Sussex. A 50-feet deep, bomb-proof concrete bunker was specially constructed, in 1941, at 620 feet above sea level.

The 500 kilowatt equipment, the most powerful in the world, had been made for Station WJZ in New Jersey. Its intended civilian use had been vetoed by the Federal Communications Commission, because the signal strength went far beyond what was considered appropriate, for commercial radio. Costing £165,000, including adaptations, it was acquired by Colonel Richard Gambier-Perry, head of Section VIII of the Secret Intelligence Service, MI6. Aspidistra was a reference to Gracie Fields and her song entitled *The Biggest Aspidistra in the World*.

American equipment on show at Blandford also includes the first hand-held mobile radio which soon became known as 'the walkie talkie'. Having a range of about a mile, the SCR-536 was the first portable RT set, designed for infantry use in the field.

Also on display is the Converter M-209B, the Hagelin Cipher Machine, which was a neat hand-operated, tape-printing device designed for rapid encipherment and deciphering of messages. It came in a canvas case and was used for clandestine operations. Though operated mechanically it did require a battery as well.

Other items on display include Transmitter BC 61OE of the United States Signal Corps and Transmitter ET4336 manufactured by the Radio Corporation of America. A Canadian No. 9 wireless set, from 1935 to 1941, was used in armoured vehicles.

Receiver HRO RO6 was a highly sensitive piece of American equipment used for radio interceptions. It is represented in the museum by the actual apparatus used by Field-Marshal Sir Bernard Montgomery's signals staff. In the first week of May in 1945, on Luneburg Heath, they used it to monitor German surrender signals. These confirmed observance in the field of the agreement, sealed at Montgomery's headquarters, which brought about the end of the war in Europe.

Adam Forty of the Royal Signals Museum with the first American Walkie Talkie radio and the ubiquitous Willys Jeep carrying the 1944 invasion star of the war in Europe.

American-made transmitter and radio receiver, as used in the 'Secret War' by the Y-Service and Special Operations Executive, displayed at Blandford Camp.

D-Day deception equipment (right) successfully deployed in Kent to confuse the Germans by pretending that the fictitious First United States Army was preparing to attack the Pas de Calais – confirming Hitler's unfounded expectations – and the Chicago-made Hallicrafters AR8-8D receiver (left).

High frequency National Receiver HRO-M made by the National Company of Malden, Massachusetts, used at Field-Marshal Montgomery's headquarters on Luneburg Heath to intercept German surrender signals confirming that the war in Europe was over.

BOCKHAMPTON

Hardy's American Monument

Higher Bockhampton – SY 728 925

The American Monument to novelist and poet Thomas Hardy (1840–1928) can be found beneath beech trees in Black Bottom at Higher Bockhampton. It stands at the end of the lane, immediately beyond Hardy's Cottage birthplace, which has been a National Trust property since 1948. The granite obelisk carries the following inscription:

'*Thomas Hardy O.M.* [Order of Merit]. *Was born in the adjacent cottage 2nd June 1840 and in it wrote* Under the Greenwood Tree *and* Far from the Madding Crowd. *This monument is erected to his memory by a few of his American admirers, 1931.*'

Hardy was as popular in New York as London, and benefited hugely from copyright protection agreements and legislation for which he had lobbied, being one of the first international celebrity authors.

Dorset novelist and poet Thomas Hardy (1840–1928) was truly international, being as well read in New York as in London.

The American Monument below beech trees behind Hardy's Cottage birthplace at Higher Bockhampton, Stinsford.

BOURNEMOUTH

Henry James

Southcliff Road – SZ 088 907

and Robert Louis Stevenson

Skerryvore – SZ 069 911

American novelist Henry James (1843–1916) who moved from New York to London, stayed in Bournemouth for three months. He stayed at St Albans, Southcliff Road, from 18 April to 30 June 1885 and visited Robert Louis Stevenson (1850–94), the author of *Treasure Island*, who had just moved into Skerryvore, previously known as Sea View, at 61 Alum Chine Road, Westbourne. Skerryvore was named for the lighthouse built by the family firm of civil engineers on an isolated rock 14 miles out into the Atlantic from Tyree.

James was completing *The Bostonians*. He dismissed Stevenson as a 'shirt-collarless Bohemian poseur' and the compliment was reciprocated by R.L.S. writing a poem in which James features as a 'bland Colossus'. Henry James was not best pleased with either the author or the setting, seeing in Victorian Bournemouth the urbanised sameness that Norman Mailer denounced as 'airport modern' a century later. 'Bournemouth,' James thundered, 'has an almost American newness and ugliness.' Its single saving grace was the view across to the Isle of Wight, looking like 'a pretty marble toy on an ultramarine horizon'.

Fanny Stevenson got on much better with James and delighted in his company, smoothing the literary relationship and encouraging his return to Bournemouth the following year. R.L.S. now writes of James's gift to them of a 'Magic Mirror' from Venice in which they visualise the reflection of the kindly face 'of a friend entwined' and elevate him in purple prose: 'The Prince of men, Henry James shall come again.' He did

return, but after Stevenson's departure and death, with typist Miss McAlpine for a stay at the Royal Bath Hotel, in 1897.

Robert Louis Stevenson was visited by American financier Charles Stebbins Fairchild (1842–1924) on Queen Victoria's golden jubilee day in 1887, for a memorably shambolic dinner at Skerryvore. Fairchild was the newly-appointed United States Secretary of the Treasury. He told Stevenson that *Dr Jekyll and Mr Hyde* was now the best selling book in New York and persuaded the author to cross the Atlantic.

Stevenson went on a boating expedition off Manasquan, New Jersey, from March to May 1888 and set about revising and rewriting a black comedy which had been produced by his stepson, Lloyd Osbourne, entitled *The Wrong Box*. The resultant easy read, which became an hilarious film in the early 1960s, perplexed the *Dictionary of National Biography*:

'The fact that the farce turns on the misadventures of a corpse caused most readers to think the levity more apparent than the judgment; but the book cannot be read without laughter.'

Stevenson's next and last great adventure was a yachting tour of the South Seas. The family set off from San Francisco with Captain Otis, on the schooner *Casco*, on 26 June 1888. The itinerary included the Paumotus Archipelago, Tahiti, and Hawaii. They set off again, from Honolulu in the trading schooner *Equator*, in June 1889. Via the Gilberts and Samoa, this took them to Sydney, but here city life immediately triggered Stevenson's chronic chest condition, and they returned to Samoa on the steamer *Janet Nicoll* 'under the most ungodly circumstances'.

Once again, despite buying a small house and 400 acres of mountain named Vailima, above Apia, he visited islands from Penrhyn and the Marshall group to New Caledonia. Tusitala, 'the teller of tales' as the natives called him, became the centre of an iconic cargo cult once his mother and their belongings from Bournemouth arrived at Vailima in the spring of 1891. Returning to civilisation, on visits to Auckland and Sydney, once again took their toll but he contin-

ued to write each day and was able to complete *David Balfour*, in serial form (entitled *Catriona* as the book), as the sequel to his Bournemouth-written Scottish classic, *Kidnapped*.

Stevenson collapsed with a brain haemorrhage on a forest walk at Vailima, and died two hours later, on the afternoon of 3 December 1894. His former house in Alum Chine Road, Bournemouth, was hit by a German bomb on 15 November 1940 and its site cleared, for a memorial garden, in 1954. Flower beds mark the lines of the walls and there is a model of the Skerryvore lighthouse.

The memorial to Robert Louis Stevenson at the site of his Bournemouth home.

Model of the Skerryvore lighthouse in the garden of Stevenson's home at Westbourne.

Major-General Richard Clement Moody

St Peter's churchyard – SZ 089 912

Former Royal Engineer and colonial Governor Major-General Richard Clement Moody (1813–87) retired to Lyme Regis. He was the first governor of the Falkland Islands, embarking on 1 October 1841, but made his name as lieutenant-governor and chief commissioner of lands and works in British Columbia. He finalised the route for the Canadian Pacific Railroad

which named Port Moody in his honour. He also planned the building of New Westminster.

Moody died whilst on holiday, of apoplexy at the Bath Hotel, Bournemouth, on 31 March 1887. He is buried above the town's 'Mother Church' in St Peter's churchyard, Hinton Road.

BOURNEMOUTH

Phyllis Bottome

Hinton Road – SZ 089 911

The novelist Phyllis Bottome (1884–1963) began her teens with a year in Bournemouth. She was the English-born daughter of a New York clergyman, Revd William Macdonald Bottome, who had come across the Atlantic to work as a country parson. He came to Bournemouth to deputise as senior curate at St Peter's Church, Hinton Road, where, with active competition from Phyllis, he 'preached the curates and even the vicar off their legs'.

The Bottome family lived in The Quadrant opposite the church. Phyllis compared the three junior curates with 'the flowers and fruit of California, so large, so luscious, so bright and vivid were the prosperous and pleasant young men! Everyone wanted the Bournemouth curates.'

Phyllis's grandmother was Margaret Bottome, the philanthropic writer who founded the King's Daughters Society of the United States of America. Phyllis Bottome entered the literary world in 1905 with *Raw Material* and later, through relief work in Vienna after the Great War she gathered the experiences that were moulded into *Old Wine*. Her other books include *Private Worlds* (1934), *Level Crossing* (1936), *Danger Signal* (1939) and *London Pride* (1941).

In 1917 she married Captain A. Ernan Forbes Dennis, the grandson of General Sir John Forbes from Inverernan, in Scotland's Grampian Mountains, and the couple settled in Hampstead.

Kenneth Hopkins

Southcote Road – SY 101 919

Poet and builder's merchant Kenneth Hopkins, the son of a Bournemouth cobbler on military service in India, was born on 7 December 1914. At the age of ten, in 1925, he achieved his first published poem, in St Peter's Church magazine. He was a choir-boy and lived on the north side of Southcote Road, close to the Central Station and has described his life there, on the edge of Bournemouth's first artisan suburb:

'Our part of Southcote Road contained bigger houses than the station end, and none of those commercial yards backing on to the railway behind our houses. In fact we backed onto the Tram depot, and the railway lay beyond that. So we felt (anyway, I did) that ours was a very select area.'

Kenneth Hopkins was born at No. 133 Southcote Road but lived mainly at No. 41, as a baby during the Great War, then stayed each night at Aunt Ada's in No. 49, before his father returned from the conflict and bought No. 125. This house was distinguished by its large eucalyptus tree and remained the family home into the second half of the twentieth century, long after Kenneth had left for London, in 1938.

Departing from his High Church roots, Kenneth Hopkins became one of the 'long-haired devotees' of occultist Aleister Crowley, but is better remembered in the town for his rallying cry for the 13th Bournemouth Boy Scouts:

'The 13th is the oldest troop that the town has ever known. T'was started soon after the seeds, by Baden Powell, were sown.'

Even in London he needed the day job, in a mobile laundry, before entering his chosen subject via bookseller Bertram Rota in 1943 and becoming a literary editor, in Fleet Street, for *Everybody's World*. He was eventually able to earn a living teaching and writing, at Liss, near Petersfield, Hampshire, in 1954, and on lecture trips around American Universities, leading to a residential term each year in the Southern Illinois University. He remained prolific, with 34 entries under his own name, 13 pseudonymous, and 25 works which he introduced or edited, listed in his first bibliographical checklist of 1961.

General Dwight D. Eisenhower

Carlton Hotel – SZ 096 910

As the whole of Dorset became an armed camp for 80,000 men of the United States Army, who were to use Portland and Weymouth as the springboard for Omaha Beach and the bloodiest of the Normandy landings, the spate of requisitions included many of the larger South Coast country houses, hotels and schools.

Several prominent Bournemouth buildings became war casualties to German bombing, with the Central Hotel on Richmond Hill and the Hotel Metropole at the Lansdowne being devastated in a Sunday lunchtime attack on 23 May 1943. The Metropole was packed with Canadian airmen, many of whom were killed or badly injured. This huge six-storey building occupied the triangle between Holdenhurst Road and Christchurch Road and has been replaced by shops and offices.

The town's great survivor is the Carlton Hotel on the East Cliff which in February 1944 hosted the American Forces Bureau of Investigation and crews of self-propelled guns when it resumed a touch of pre-war style to welcome General Dwight D. Eisenhower, the Supreme Commander Allied Forces Western Europe and future President of the United States of the America.

General Eisenhower, with key staff officers and General Sir Bernard Montgomery, who was effectively commander-in-chief of Allied land forces, came to Bournemouth to discuss and approve the final master plan for the invasion of Europe. Across the bay, joined by King George VI on 18 April 1944, they watched the Exercise Smash live-fire rehearsals from Fort Henry on Redend Point at Studland.

Invasion talk at the Carlton Hotel, Bournemouth, between General Dwight D. Eisenhower (left), the Supreme Commander of Allied Forces, and General Sir Bernard Montgomery in February 1944.

BOURNEMOUTH

Hal Geneen

West Cliff Road — SZ 080 907

American tycoon Harold S. Geneen (1910–97), who turned International Telephone and Telegraph into a global giant, pledged $400,000 towards the San Diego Convention and Richard Nixon's continued tenure of the White House in 1972. He was born, 'improbably enough' as the feature writers put it, in Bournemouth, where the family were staying, in West Cliff Road. They were only in England for a year, that of 1910, before his Russian father and Italian mother left for America.

Young Hal was devoted to his mother, who brought him up in Connecticut after her marriage broke up, and commemorated her in London with a teak bench in the gardens opposite the Connaught Hotel:

'In memory of Ada Geneen, who loved the gardens of her native England, from her son Harold S. Geneen.'

Geneen was propelled into scandal when Washington columnist Jack Anderson printed a secret memo – 'please destroy this, huh?' – in which President Nixon, Attorney-General John Mitchell and henchmen Ed Reinecke and Bob Haldeman were implicated in a conspiratorial fix of an anti-trust case against ITT. Lobbyist Mrs Dita Beard, writing to ITT's Washington chief Bill Merriam, had disclosed that 'our noble commitment has gone a long way toward our negotiations on mergers eventually coming out as Hal wants them ... We all know Hal and his big mouth.'

BOVINGTON

Armoured Fighting Vehicles

Tank Museum – SY 830 883

Bovington Camp, near Wool, is home to both the headquarters of the Royal Armoured Corps and its Tank Museum. Tank training and testing has been going on here since the development of the world's first tanks during the Great War. Since then, armoured fighting vehicles from armies across the globe have been brought to Bovington for evaluation. Many of these have found their way into the Tank Museum which was founded in 1926 after an inspired sugges-tion by the author and poet Rudyard Kipling. It has grown into a uniquely fascinating complex full of mili-tary hardware and history.

American fighting vehicles are well represented. *Michael* is the oldest surviving Sherman tank. This and other perfectly preserved examples of United States and Canadian armour include the following which are described in alphabetical order.

Boarhound T18

General Motors designed this armoured car especially for the use of the British Army in the Second World War. A mammoth of a vehicle, the Boarhound was intended for desert use, though in the event the war had moved on and it was not used very much.

Cromwell Cruiser RAM Mark III

The Canadian-built Cruiser was originally modelled on the General Lee. They were issued to reconnaissance regiments in the armoured divisions. The exception were the 7th Division who used Cruisers in all their armoured regiments.

Boarhound T18 armoured car.

DUKW-353

This tank was designed in New York by Sparkman and Stephens. DUKW as a name has nothing to do with ducks, though the similarity in sounds is a convenient coincidence. It is in fact an acronym – D stands for 1942 (the year it was put into production by General Motors). U means Utility, implying that the tank was an amphibious vehicle. K meant All-wheel Drive. W stood for Twin rear axles. 'One of the great successes of D-Day,' as it is described on the information panels, DUKWs brought supplies ashore and closely followed the invading assault troops. Even when the Mulberry Harbours were operating at full efficiency, they still brought in less supplies than the DUKWs. The DUKW had a powerful 94-horsepower engine which gave it a land speed of 80 kilometres per hour (50 miles per hour).

DUKW-353 amphibious truck.

General Chaffee

Light tank named after General Adna R. Chaffee, chief of United States Armored Forces in 1940. It was supplied to at least 24 countries and saw service across Asia from the Middle East to Indo-China.

General Chaffee tank.

General Grant M3

Medium tank, built in 1942. It was built by the Americans, intended for British use, but also bought by the Canadians. The Grant's turret was of British design but the rest of the vehicle was American. The General Grant weighed 28 tons, had a maximum armour thickness of 57 millimetres and possessed a 340-horsepower radial engine, giving a top land speed of 26 miles per hour. Its potential range of action reached 144 miles.

General Grant M3 tank.

General Patton Series: M46, M47, M48

Medium tanks which went into action in the Korean War. They were revamped editions of the Pershing which had gone into the field, in central Europe, during the final battles of the Second World War. The M46 was decidedly inferior when compared to the British Centurion tanks, then on the drawing board for production in 1951, so work began on a Mark II edition, designated the M47. This first appeared in 1948 and was used in the armies of Germany, France, Italy, Spain, Japan and many others. The final Patton, the M48, was produced in 1953 and saw action in the Middle East and in Vietnam.

Above: *Tiger's jaws on General Patton M46 tank.*

Left: *General Patton M48 tank.*

General Stuart Mark IV British 'Honey'

Light tank, the sixth of its kind to be tested, was put into production in 1941, and issued in quantity to the British. Christened the General Stuart – for Confederate General J.E.B. 'Jeb' Stuart – it was outclassed by most enemy tanks at the time, and therefore went into service use for forward reconnaissance purposes rather than as a fighting vehicle. Some regiments removed the turret and used it as a mobile gun carrier. The British 'Honey' model differed from the American Hothead in being lighter with small windows on either side of the turret.

General Stuart Mark IV British-issued 'Honey' light tank.

General Stuart Mark IV US 'Hothead'

A heavier, American brand of the Mark IV Stuart. It was slightly taller than the Mark IV 'Honey' and had blotches of camouflage for reconnaissance missions.

General Stuart US-issued 'Hothead' light tank.

Heavy Assault Tank T14

This tank was only ever produced as a prototype. By the time it was ready for mass production, in 1943, the ubiquitous Sherman tank rendered it obsolete.

Heavy Assault Tank T14.

Kangaroo

Canadian armoured personnel carrier with low lines to protect those inside.

Kangaroo from Canada.

M8 Greyhound

Armoured car built to be used in the US Army, but was scrapped quite quickly due to its vulnerability, with both open turret and light armour.

M8 Greyhound armoured car.

M9A1 Half-Track

This lightly armoured car was one of the most versatile vehicles used by the Allies from D-Day onwards. They were useful as infantry transport, radio vehicles, repair trucks and armoured ambulances.

M9-A1 Half-Track.

M10 Tank Destroyer

Self-propelled guns that were used by the anti-tank regiments of the Royal Artillery. In action from D-Day onwards, many M10s carried an American three-inch gun, but these were gradually upgraded with British 17-pounders.

M10 Tank Destroyer.

M22 'Locust'

The American M22 light tank was designed and developed in 1941–42 to provide armoured support for airborne forces. Named 'Locust' by the British, being carried in Hamilcar gliders (one at a time) towed by a Halifax tug-plane, its combat debut was with the 8th Airborne Division in the Rhine crossing of 22 March 1945.

M22 Locust light tank.

M60-A1

This American medium tank was developed from the General Patton M48 in 1958. Weighing 46 tons, it mounted a British-designed 105-mm gun, and went into production in 1960.

M60-A1 tank.

M103-A2

Having no actual name, this tank was designed to accompany infantry soldiers. It was a reasonably effective wartime design though not put into production until 1956, long after the end of the Korean War.

Pershing

Heavy tanks, equipped with 90-mm guns, used for front-line reconnaissance. After the Second World War, 2000 Pershings were taken from storage, remodelled, reissued and renamed, as General Pattons.

Above: *Pershing tank.*

Below: *Manikin of General George Patton* (left), *in the jeep, with a Pershing crew during the breakout from Normandy.*

M103-A2 tank.

Sherman Duplex Drive

These 'swimming tanks' were the first to land on D-Day. They had a large canvas skirt to help buoy them up, and were equipped with emergency scuba gear of a sort, should there be a problem. They were carried to all five invasion beaches though due to rough seas and most being launched too far out, few of them successfully swam ashore.

Sherman M4A1 *(Michael)*

The oldest surviving specimen of this famous tank, anywhere in the world, The first to be shipped across the Atlantic, under the terms of the Lend-Lease Act 1942, it was named *Michael* for Michael Dewar, head of the British Tank Mission to Washington DC. The prototype was brought back for trials on the Lulworth Ranges in the middle of the war, before the mass importation of American Armour (or Armor, rather) in preparation for the invasion of Europe. *Michael* appeared in Horseguards' Parade, on display, as the first Lend-Lease Sherman tank.

Left: *Sherman Duplex Drive amphibious tank, named for the rear propellers in its skirt.*

Below: *Sherman M4-A1 tank, named* Michael.

Sherman V Crab Flail

Although American in origin, this tank was adapted for British use by London bus builders AEC, who added an extra gearbox for manoeuvrability. One of its main uses was to clear mines, with flail attachments to detonate them. It was also used by regiments such as the 2nd Dragoons and the Westminster Dragoons. Sherman Crabs went ahead of the D-Day tanks, protected by their cover fire, in order to clear mine-strewn roads behind the beaches.

Sherman Crab Flail.

Staghound

Armoured troop carrier, American in design, created for British and Canadian use. Though roomy, size can be a disadvantage in war, because they were too large to hide and also difficult to turn in narrow lanes. Therefore they rarely reached the front-line. Instead they were often purloined by regimental commanders for tactical headquarters.

Staghound armoured car.

Weasel

Heavy troop carrier, associated with the enigmatic American genius Geoffrey Pyke though it is uncertain whether he actually designed the tank. Effective on difficult terrain, such as mud, sand and snow, groups of Weasels were often dispatched to deserts and swamps, and taken on polar expeditions.

Weasel tracked carrier.

White Scout Car M3

Armoured car, designed for use alongside tanks. Despite this, it was slightly too big for a scout car and was adapted for other purposes by all Allied armies. Some became a desirable command vehicle for senior officers.

M3 White Scout Car.

BROWNSEA ISLAND

Sir Augustus Foster

Branksea Castle — SZ 031 877

Branksea Castle stands on Brownsea Island. Now owned by the National Trust, the main island in the middle of Poole Harbour is reached by summertime ferries from Poole Quay and Sandbanks. It was bought by Sir Augustus Foster (1780–1848) in 1840.

Augustus John Foster was born on 1 December 1780. Through the influence of his mother, re-married to the 5th Duke of Devonshire, he found a career as a civil servant and was appointed Secretary to the British Legation in Naples. From there he received a sensitive major appointment that was beyond his abilities and in which he proved to be a disaster. Foster embarked in August 1811 for Washington to serve as Minister Plenipotentiary on behalf of the Court of St James to the United States of America.

In temperament he was not a diplomat at all and he failed to sort out a simmering row over the impressment of American seamen into the Royal Navy for the war against France. America had seized its independence in the war of 1775–81, and felt that her neutrality was being compromised. Foster was arrogant and belligerent in his defence of King George III's Orders in Council, signed in 1807, that had brought about the dispute. Matters came to a head in June 1812.

Foster failed to hold the situation at a time when in reality there was no longer any dispute. London had backed down on 16 June and withdrawn the contentious orders. Washington was unaware of any such conciliatory mood, as none was apparent in our minister, and declared war against the British on the 18th. America prepared to invade Canada. That offensive was outmanoeuvred and British troops in North America came south to burn the Capitol and destroy most of the Library of Congress.

The great American victory of the war did not come about until 1815, and then two weeks after the Treaty of Ghent had ended the hostilities. Jean Laffite, the French pirate, had tipped off the defenders of New Orleans about imminent seaborne landings, which were then decisively countered with 700 British dead and 1400 British wounded, for the loss of 8 American dead and 13 American wounded. As for Foster, having won his place in history as the last man to put us at war with the United States of America, his continuation of diplomacy by other means was met with the standard protocol; he was sent packing. Back in England he entered Parliament, as MP for Cockermouth, and in May 1814 was at sea again, to Copenhagen as Minister Plenipotentiary to Denmark. This was a posting of no consequence — which was why he was given it — and Foster settled down to married life with Albinia Jane Hobart and in 1822 was appointed to the Privy Council. In 1824 he was posted to Turin and received a knighthood the following year.

Foster avoided starting another war and London left him in Italy for sixteen years. This period of acceptable if lack-lustre conduct was rewarded with a baronetcy and on retirement in 1840 he bought Brownsea Island from Sir Charles Chad.

Far from finding paradise he fell into bouts of deep depression. These steadily became more intense as his general health deteriorated. The last was on 1 August 1848 when he was at home in Branksea Castle — the contemporary form of the island's name — and he ended it by slitting his throat. *The Gentleman's Magazine* records:

'Sir Augustus Foster, Bt. At an inquest held on the body of the deceased, it appeared that he had for several months been

suffering from disease of the heart and lungs, and had recently laboured under delirium, during a fit of which he destroyed himself by cutting his throat. A verdict was returned of a temporary insanity.'

His widow stayed on the island and the next era began with a visit from Colonel and Mrs William Petrie Waugh, late of the XXth (East Devonshire) Regiment of Foot and the Indian Army, in 1853.

BRYANSTON

Wystan Hugh Auden

Bryanston School – ST 870 074

Before he left for New York, the poet Wystan Hugh Auden (1907–73) was an English master at Bryanston School, near Blandford. During his time, in the 1930s, the teachers judged the boys in a beauty contest. A former pupil later recalled 'plenty' of physical and platonic relationships in the school in Auden's time.

Auden became a Republican stretcher-bearer in the Spanish Civil War. His existential conflict with 'the claustrophobia and cosiness' of English society was put on hold in 1939 when he left for the United States. He became an American citizen and his continuing search for salvation put him back in contact with religion. Friends such as Stephen Spender doubted if he would ever return to England but Auden came home as soon as the war was over. Edmund Wilson recalled his reappearance in 1945:

'Without showing the least embarrassment, he complained about the coldness of English houses, and of other hardships of life in England, and told them that London hadn't really been bombed. They were speechless with indignation. He also assured them – being a homosexual chauvinist – that General Eisenhower was queer. I love this story, because the English are such experts at putting other people down, that it is wonderful to see an expatriate Britisher coming back and working out on the boys at home.'

Auden reviewed the memoirs of Evelyn Waugh and Leonard Woolf in *The New Yorker* of 3 April 1965. Before the war Auden was instrumental in propelling the emotional development of the young composer Benjamin Britten, who also attended Gresham's School at Holt, when they worked together on documentary films. Many of the longest lasting memories of Auden on both sides of the Atlantic concerned his eccentricities in the bedroom which included a tendency to gather his host's coats, newspapers and stair-carpet for use as bedding.

BURTON BRADSTOCK

GI photo-call

Village settings – SY 490 890

All changed with Dorset's planned contribution to D-Day on Sunday 16 April 1944. That day the Allied High Command decided to relocate British invasion Force G (for Gold) eastwards to the harbours and inlets of the Solent and Southampton Water. In their place, as at Freshwater holiday camp on the seaside near Burton Bradstock and Bradford Down Camp in woods above Bradford Peverell, came United States Force O (for Omaha). As a result their target beaches were also transposed, with the Americans being tasked to land on what was now designated Omaha Beach, and the British troops to take the next sector to the east, codenamed Gold Beach.

The Supreme Commander, General Dwight D. Eisenhower visited the main Dorset encampments, as did at least one photographer attached to the 'Fighting Firsts' or 'Big Red One' as America's famous First Infantry Division is known from its badge. The Commanding General, Major-General Clarence R. Huebner moved his Divisional Headquarters to Langton House, in parkland at Langton Long Blandford, and had at his command 34,142 men and 3306 vehicles. Another 50,000 men arrived in Dorset with support and back-up units.

Captain J. J. McGlynn of the United States Navy was given responsibility for the shipment of V Corps of the First United States Army. Commanded by General Leonard 'Gee' Gerow, V Corps comprised the 1st US Infantry Division, the 2nd US Infantry Division, the 2nd US Armored Division, and two elite Ranger battalions. Their departure was put in the hands of the 14th Major Port of the United States Transportation Corps, manning Dorset ports from West Bay to Poole and centred on Advanced Amphibious Base Weymouth and Portland.

The photographic file from Burton Bradstock, with village locations having been identified by the author from copies supplied by the National Archives in Washington three decades ago, is remarkable in its scale and scope. It cleverly bridges cultural divides, imagined or real, and subtly places the American arrivals into the context of a stable English community that shares common aspirations and roots.

Revd Arthur Dittmer (left) *and American officers being treated to a display of country dancing by Burton Bradstock schoolchildren.*

Under the sycamore tree on the green at Burton Bradstock, village children show off a machine-gun belt washed up on the Chesil Beach, to GIs John L. Lawson of Port Jervis, New York, Robert S. Hastings of Azusa, California, Leo H. Pearson of Springfield, New York, and Corporal Roland Henry of Holland, Pennsylvania.

The wartime caption to this picture of a pillbox on the Chesil Beach read: 'In 1940 the beach was guarded against invasion, first by Local Defence Volunteers, then by the Home Guard. Today, with the tables turned, United States troops can spend their leisure hours on it. Sitting on a concrete blockhouse, behind which Britain's amateur ill-armed soldiers were prepared to sell their lives dearly, Corporal Bert Markowitz of Astoria, Queen's, New York City, plays his violin. Markowitz was a student at the University of Miami and played with the National Broadcasting Corporation as a studio musician. Listening to him is G. R. Miller of Louisville, Kentucky.'

Eyes towards France, from the Chesil Beach, as American GIs turned south Dorset into a colossal armed camp and prepared to take the war back across the Channel.

Looking one's best for war at an open-air hair salon on a boulder in the pea-shingle.

Roy St Jean, from Springfield, Massachusetts, asks the way to the canteen. Petty Officer Podger, who was born in Burton Bradstock, had been recently invalided out of the Royal Navy after serving through both world wars.

The Burton Bradstock blacksmith, appropriately named Benjamin Burton, turns a hoof towards the Americans. 'US troops are discovering that the Britisher is not as stand-offish as he is said to be,' the contemporary caption read.

Benjamin Burton with senior American officers at the Smithy in Burton Bradstock. The Master Sergeant (centre) has a plaster across a recent wound to his forehead.

The GI offensive began in the Dove Inn at Southover, Burton Bradstock. Their pint was beer – darker but less potent than the rough cider of the locals. The poster for H. and G. Simmonds at Reading was deliberate disinformation, though the company had a depot at Blandford, as the Germans were being led to believe that the invasion was coming from much further east. Another poster makes an appeal on behalf of prisoners of war and the Simmonds' calendar shows the month of April in 1944.

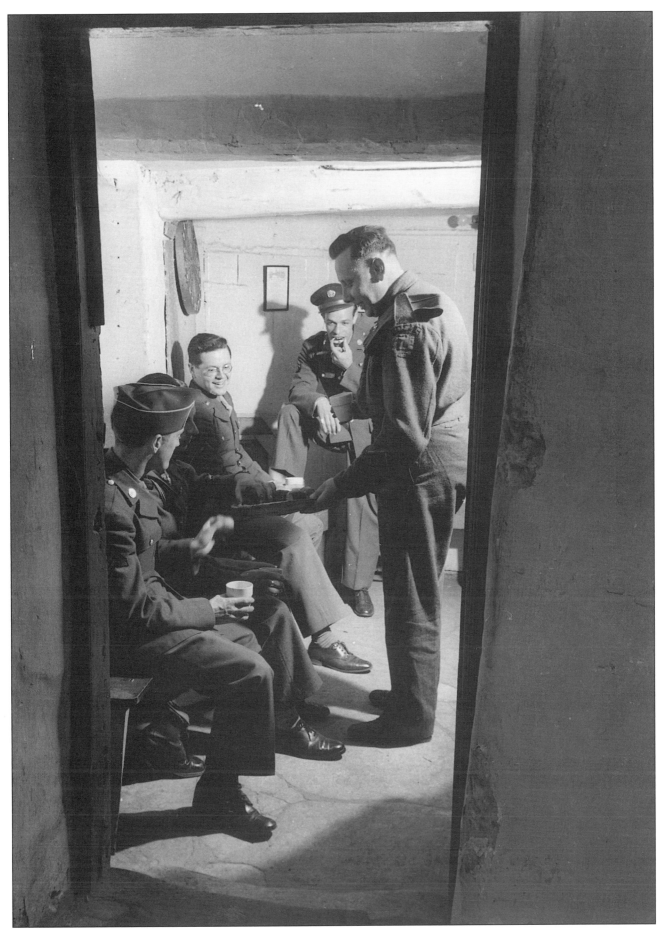

Gunner Weightman of the Royal Artillery, described as 'an old habitué', handing round home-made cakes in the village canteen to Corporal James Flower of Walpole, Massachusetts, Private first-class Roy St Jean of Springfield, Mass., and Corporal Allan Decker of Chicago.

Cocoa in NAAFI cups to bridge an ocean and a generation gap. Corporal David W. Roberts, from Iowa, leans out of his holiday camp billet at Freshwater, Burton Bradstock, to chat to Betty 'Freckles' Mackay, a London evacuee from the Blitz days, and local boy Chris Kerley.

Common culture is the theme of this propaganda photograph. The subtle inference lies in the date of the table-tomb at Burton Bradstock, because before 1783 the two nations share their history. The rector, Revd Arthur Dittmer, points this out to Major E. M. Beebe of Burlington, Vermont, and Lieutenant S. M. Weitzner of Ridgewood, New York.

Above: *Village boy Barry Knell manning A. E. Cheney's pumps at the local gas station – the Red House Garage between Burton Bradstock and Southover – as another lad cleans the windscreen of a Willys Jeep. The importance of the photo-call is shown by the fact that this carries a 'Headquarters' emblem. Behind the thatched cottage is the village playing field and the church tower is in the distance.*

Left: *On cue, one guesses, cattle came into view to add a bucolic touch.*

Sergeant Harold D. Kregar, from Cheyenne Wells, Colorado, who won the Legion of Merit in Iceland, having tea at Burton Bradstock with the wife of the village schoolmaster.

St Mary's Church, Burton Bradstock, from the Rectory lawn. Tea was hosted by Revd and Mrs Arthur Dittmer and the tabby cat. Their United States Army guests were Lieutenant S. M. Weitzner of Ridgewood, New York, and Major S. M. Beebe of Burlington, Vermont.

CERNE ABBAS

Thomas Notley

The Royal Oak – ST 666 013

Positioned in the market place at Cerne Abbas, the thatched Royal Oak dates from the 1540s and is a rarity among the many public houses carrying the name, as it stands beside what was in all probability the actual route used by King Charles II as he fled in disguise to the continent after defeat at the Battle of Worcester in September 1651.

The Royal Oak was owned at the time by the Notley family. There are brass memorials, set in stone in the central aisle of the parish church to John Notley senior who died in 1612 and John Notley junior who died in 1626. The fourth son of a third John Notley, namely Thomas Notley who was born in 1634, became a London lawyer and emigrated to Maryland in 1662. He was a friend of Charles Calvert who the previous year had succeeded his father, Cecil Calvert, as Governor of Maryland.

Thomas Notley flourished in Maryland, as an attorney, merchant, landowner and planter. He purchased 1500 acres at Basford Manor, beside the Wicomico River, and offered land in the vicinity of the first fort at St Mary's City to the Maryland authorities on apppointment as Deputy Governor. In November 1670, Notley bought by barter – the price being 40,000 pounds of tobacco – 1800 acres of land north of the Annacostia River in Charles County. Title, in the form of proprietorial deed of patent, was passed to him by Lord Baltimore who had dispossessed the Powhatan tribe of Algonquin Indians.

The signifance of this purchase is that it included Jenkins' Hill which is now known to the world as Capitol Hill. For a time, however, it took the name Cern Abbey Manor, as a reminder of the Benedictine ruin back home, a fireplace and other features from which can be seen to this day incorporated into the Royal Oak and other post-monastic buildings in Cerne Abbas, Dorset. Abbas, incidentally, means 'Father' which was the form of address for its abbot.

Cern Abbey Manor, a collective estate name for all Notley's real estate in Charles County, was bequeathed to his godson Notley Rozier, the son of his close friend Benjamin Rozier, on Thomas's death in 1678. By 1791 it had passed to Notley Young, who built a brick house high above the Potomac River in 1756, and Charles Carroll who signed the Declaration of Independence in 1776.

The choice of Jenkins' Hill for the capital of the American federal government came about in February 1791 as a result of a suggestion by President Washington's boundary commissioner, Daniel Carroll, cousin of Charles Carroll. Notley Young and Daniel Carroll opened negotiations for providing land for the Congress House and an agreement was signed on 30 March 1791, bringing in adjoining landowners, to establish 'a Federal City' with the ground being divided into alternate lots of equal value, one being ceded to the government and the next retained by the proprietors.

Daniel Carroll built an impressive house on the south side of what was being transformed into Capitol Hill and another of his ventures was to provide the principal tavern for congressmen, on a lot facing First Street. This was built in 1799 and was open for business when Congress arrived in what was now Washington in the autumn of 1800.

Robert Davis, Kerry and Romany (the buzzard) sharing a pint at the Royal Oak in Cerne Abbas.

The Market Place in Cerne Abbas, where the Notley family owned property, has direct links with the establishment of Capitol Hill and the founding of Washington DC.

The Royal Oak (right) and mediaeval Abbey Street (left) in Cerne Abbas.

CHETTLE

Revd John West

Chettle House and Church – SU 952 133

This English baroque mansion in the rolling foothills of Cranborne Chase, between Tarrant Hinton and Farnham, was the home of Revd John West (1778–1845). He was also rector of the church in its grounds, but is now better remembered in Canada than Chettle.

West was appointed chaplain to the Hudson's Bay Company and became the first missionary to the North American Indians, on behalf of the Church Missionary Society, between 1820 and 1828. His Red River settlement church and school are now St John's Cathedral, Winnipeg.

On returning to Dorset, he wrote *A Brief Memoir of William B …* to commemorate a twelve-year-old who died at Chettle, in 1831. This was joined by a 246-page biography devoted to his late wife, Harriet West (1789–1839), which appeared as *A Memoir of Mrs John West* in 1840. John West regarded her as a saint, and his inspiration in the adjoining parish of Farnham, where as rector from 1834 he devoted the remainder of his life to the teaching and welfare of deprived children. His final good work in Dorset was a scheme for a Gypsy School between Chettle and Farnham in buildings that later became – also relatively short-lived – the Pitt-Rivers Museum.

Chettle House, an exemplar of its kind in the rolling foothills of Cranborne Chase, is a perfect Queen Anne style mansion that was designed by Thomas Archer (died 1743). A pupil of Sir John Vanbrugh, he worked for Queen Anne, George I, and George II, and created a large number of important buildings, including St John's Church, Westminster.

Peter Wayne, the leading modern authority on Archer and his architecture, came upon his passion while being detained at Government expense. He had escaped from an English jail and found refuge in an Archer church. Inspired by the premier architect of the English baroque, to the extent of fanaticism, Wayne studied at Long Lartin open prison and proceeded to put all available information on computer.

It was as a prisoner on parole that Peter Wayne came to Chettle House as the star performer at a conference, which featured his dissertation on the architect and his work, for owners Mr and Mrs Patrick Bourke. Some years ago, in about 1996, Janet Bourke recalled the event:

'He was a born actor; a tremendous strain to be with, so exhaustingly self-opinionated and excited. A prison warden had been provided as his minder, paid for by Channel 4, who were filming it. The sad thing is that he later skipped off, running away it is said when the prison governor himself was accompanying him for an outing, and the last we heard he was back inside.'

CHRISTCHURCH

USAAF Station 416

Christchurch Advance Landing Ground – SZ 185 930

Now largely covered by housing estates, at Somerford, Christchurch Aerodrome became Christchurch Advance Landing Ground upon its designation as Station 416 of the 9th United States Army Air Force. The 405th Fighter Bomber Group, fielding Thunderbolt fighter-bombers, had docked in Liverpool with nearly a thousand officers and men. They arrived in Christchurch on 7 March 1944 and were tasked to undertake cross-Channel operations in support of the forthcoming D-Day landings.

The 405th comprised 509, 510 and 511 Squadrons of the USAAF, equipped with single-engine Republic P-47 Thunderbolt fighter-bombers.

Several of their aircraft crashed around Christchurch. One Thunderbolt crashed in the playground of Highcliffe School, fortunately empty at 19.30 hours, on 30 April 1944. The worst air-crashes of the war for Christchurch, and Dorset as a whole, occurred when Foxwood Avenue, Mudeford, was devastated by three Thunderbolts of the 509th Squadron from the 405th Fighter Bomber Group. In the first mishap on take-off, Lieutenant Vincent R. James survived, at 06.45 hours on 29 June 1944, and no one was hurt on the ground. Then at 14.00 hours the same pilot tried to lift off again. Once more he failed to gain sufficient height and this time overshot the runway into a bunga-low. His fuel tanks and bombs exploded, bringing down another Thunderbolt that was coming in to land, though its pilot was unhurt.

A total of 16 were killed and 18 injured in the accident and a subsequent explosion as a bomb went off among rescue workers. Mortally injured, Lieutenant James died that evening, in the arms of nurse Irene Stevenson in Boscombe Hospital.

The next P-47 crash was less dramatic, with a Thunderbolt landing short and coming to rest on the Lymington road, on 2 July 1944. Another lucky escape was had by men of the 306th Bombardment Group of the USAAF, crammed into Flying Fortress 866 for a recuperation trip to the seaside, which overshot the western boundary of the notoriously short Christchurch Aerodrome on 15 July 1945. It ploughed into scrubland, ripping out the near-side port engine, but came to a halt without further harm.

For the people of Christchurch the excitement, danger and noise of war were already a distant memory. During the Battle of Normandy the entire 405th Fighter Bomber Group were ordered to follow the war, and took off for Airstrip 8 at Picauville, in the Allied-occupied Cherbourg peninsula, on 11 July 1944. Flags and other memorabilia are displayed in Christchurch Priory.

Republic P-47 Thunderbolts of the United States Army Air Force, bristling with ten 5-inch rockets, as flown from Christchurch Aerodrome in the invasion months of 1944.

Above: *Oomph-girl Ann Sheridan gracing Lieutenant Curry Powell's P-47 Thunderbolt of 510 Squadron at Station 416, Christchurch, of the 9th United States Army Air Force.*

Right: *The Stars and Stripes and the Union Flag, together in Christchurch Priory as standards, from a shared RAF Christchurch.*

CORSCOMBE

Thomas Hollis

Urless Farm – ST 519 039

Fields and farms at Corscombe and Halstock carry names of North American places, persons and ideals of the eighteenth century, and most are politically loaded with the eighteenth century buzz-words of libertarian philosophy.

All were coined or adopted by gentleman scholar and book editor Thomas Hollis (1720–74) whose wealthy uncle had been the principal benefactor of Harvard University. Thomas Hollis inherited his uncle's 700 acres and carried on the good works by endowing Harvard's famous library.

He lived at Urless Farm, Corscombe, and was instrumental in rebuilding its parish church in 1746, but left instructions that he should not be interred in consecrated ground. He chose to be buried on the high southern point of his estate, at the 800 feet contour, on open ground between Urless Farm and Toller Down, in an unmarked grave at the middle of a field. Legend has it that his horse was shot and buried with him.

Harvard Farm, to the east of Sutton Bingham Reservoir at Halstock, is at the northern end of his lands. As well as financing Harvard's esteemed collection, Hollis also gave books to universities at Berne and Zurich. Locke Farm, Halstock, was in tribute of the English philosopher, John Locke. Liberty Farm pre-dates the new American nation of 1776 but carries the key word in which it would be conceived.

Hollis had tried to reason with William Pitt, the Earl of Chatham, to avoid that colonial war. Field names include the trendy catchwords Reasonableness, Comprehension and Understanding from Locke's works and one addressed to Archbishop Secker, but that was in derision, so Hollis applied it to barren ground. Secker's had proved impossible to cultivate. Massachusetts – never easy for a Brit to spell – is now abbreviated to Massy Field.

As a man of letters, Hollis was involved in the editing and publication of several major works, including Toland's *Life of Milton* (1761) and John Locke's *Two Treatises on Government* and *Letters Concerning Toleration*. Ascetic in all things, Hollis' diet excluded sugar, salt and spices. He drank only water. Urless Farm he regarded as 'a most healthy, and, I think, beautiful spot; the very earth itself is sweet beyond a nosegay'.

His friend and heir Thomas Brand became Thomas Brand-Hollis 'upon succeeding to Mr Hollis' fortune'.

Urless Farm as it was in the time of Thomas Hollis, engraved from a painting of 1747.

CREECH

Sir Oliver Lawrence

Creech Grange – SY 911 823

The elegant country house to the south of Wareham, at the foot of the Purbeck Hills, was built by Sir Oliver Lawrence, on land from the former Bindon Abbey holdings acquired after Henry VIII dissolved the monasteries in 1539.

Lawrence was an ancestor of the first American President, George Washington, and the joint arms of the two families – the famous stars and stripes of Washington's signet ring and the American flag – appear in memorials across the hill at Steeple and up the valley in Affpuddle. Creech Grange was bought by Nathaniel Bond in 1691, and remained in the Bond family for 400 years, until this part of their Purbeck estates was sold to Norman and Pat Hayward in 1990.

The home of George Washington's ancestor, Sir Oliver Lawrence, at Creech Grange in the Purbeck Hills.

CROSSWAYS

USAAF Station 454

Mount Skippet Way – SY 767 882

Most of the wartime airfield at RAF Warmwell, which became Station 454 of the 474th Fighter Group of the United States Army Air Force, has since been dug up for sand and gravel pits. These in their turn are now disappearing under the suburban streets of Crossways. The memorial to the Battle of Britain and D-Day flyers is a stone and plaque on an open space beside Mount Skippet Way.

Warmwell's heroic Spitfire pilots of the Battle of Britain included American flyer Eugene Quimby Tobin of 609 Squadron. Pilot Officer 'Red' Tobin, as he was nicknamed, had learned to fly in Los Angeles by using his wages from film-makers MGM, where he was a studio messenger, to fund his lessons. He proceeded to volunteer for what proved to be three separate conflicts, firstly in Finland in the autumn of 1939, then l'Armee de l'Air in Paris, and finally the Royal Air Force after to escaping to England from St Jean de Luz.

While serving at Warmwell, Tobin was credited with the destruction of a Messerschmitt Bf.110 on 25 August 1940 and was partly responsible for bringing down a a Dornier Do.17 bomber on 15 September. From 609 Squadron, with its other two Americans, he was the first to arrive at Church Fenton on 19 September 1940 to form what became the famous Eagle Squadron. Tobin's luck ran out a year later, when he was shot down and killed in 71 Squadron's first sweep over France, on 7 September 1941. He is buried in the eastern cemetery at Boulogne.

The grass aerodrome at RAF Warmwell later fielded 48 American Lockheed Lightning P-38J fighter-bombers of 428, 429 and 430 Squadrons from March to August 1944. They contributed to the cross-Channel offensive from Brittany to the Seine, in which they were tasked to 'hit anything that moves' in occupied France. They then flew to forward bases across the channel as the Battle of Normandy moved towards Paris.

Many pilots were killed, including Lieutenant Kimball who crashed in Dorset, near Cheselbourne on 21 May 1944. Two pilots were killed while escorting B-26 Marauders across northern France on 7 May 1944. Three pilots were killed on D-Day minus one (5 June) and others came home that day with tree branches caught up in their distinctive square-boom tails from low-level attacks on a bridge over the River Seine. Lieutenant Thacker – shot down over Normandy in the spring – surprised his mates by turning up back at Warmwell after the invasion, having escaped via Spain.

Pilot Officer 'Red' Quimby from Los Angeles, one of the American volunteers who fought in the Battle of Britain, in a Spitfire of 609 Squadron at RAF Warmwell.

Squadron Leader R. E. Morrow of 402 (Royal Canadian Air Force Squadron) astride his Hurricane Mark IIb 'Hurribomber' as it is armed at RAF Warmwell in the winter of 1941.

Whirlwind Bellows *of 263 Squadron at RAF Warmwell carried the name of Flight-Lieutenant H. K. Blackshaw but here it was on loan to twenty-two-year-old Canadian Flying Officer J. P. Coyne from Manitoba who had just been awarded the Distinguished Flying Cross.*

Canadian operations team taking over at RAF Warmwell in 1943.

Above: *Lockheed Lightnings were deployed at Warmwell for cross-Channel attacks on the Germans in occupied France.*

Right: *Beech tree graffiti, much of it American from the Second World War, beside former Warmwell Aerodrome in Knighton Heath Wood.*

DORCHESTER

Revd John White

St Peter's Church – SY 694 907

The Dorset county town ('not to be confused with Dorchester in Oxfordshire,' to quote the press officer at the American Embassy) was the home of Revd John White (1575–1648). He put a working lifetime of effort and energy into forming the Massachusetts Company and the founding and endowment of Dorchester in New England.

John White, a Welsh puritan lawyer, settled in Dorchester. Towards the end of his life, he was known as 'Century White' for chairing and publishing the Parliamentary report into alleged clerical immorality which appeared under the title *First Century of Scandalous Malignant Priests*, in 1643. His other obsessive interest was with America, though he does not appear to have crossed the Atlantic. From 1624 he actively encouraged emigration from Dorset to the New World and then helped the Massachusetts Bay colonists to gain their charter. It was procured in 1629 and appears to have been personally drafted by White.

The Pilgrim Fathers landed at Plymouth Rock, in 1620, to establish the British colony that grew into Massachusetts and became the 'Mother State' of New England. They were seeking 'the promised land' where nonconformists could worship in freedom according to their conscience. To protect their interests, and mobilise the next influx of colonists, White founded the Massachusetts Company.

This required capital of £1800. Sir Richard Saltonstall became the chief shareholder. Instalments of £200 per year were payable in London at the Royal Exchange. The Council for New England signed the patent, establishing Massachusetts as an entity, on 19 March 1628. King Charles I confirmed it by signing and sealing the charter on 4 March 1629.

John White personally chose the ministers to lead the Dorset flock. The first pair to be sent across the Atlantic were Francis Higginson (1587–1630), who sailed in the *Talbot* from Gravesend for Salem on 25 April 1629, and Samuel Skelton who left in the *George Bonaventura* on 4 May 1629. The vessels met at sea and prepared to sail together in a convoy known as 'Winthrop's Fleet'. John Winthrop himself followed in the *Arbella*.

John White boarded vessels at Plymouth to conduct services and bless the endeavour. He also gathered his own pioneering party, of 150 Dorset colonists, who sailed from Plymouth in the *Mary and John* in 1630. They called their settlement Dorchester and other Dorset men and women, from around Sherborne, established what is now the town of Sherborn, Massachusetts.

Back in England, John White continued to control the helm, in a pivotal administrative and promotional role. He acted as treasurer, juggling assets and stock, but repeatedly resisted suggestions that he should visit the new Dorchester. John Winthrop, the leader across the water, kept urging him to come. He dangled the requests in otherwise prosaic letters requesting practical supplies, such as cod-lines and hooks, but these were sent as cargo rather than being delivered by White in person. The same applied to orders for plants that could be used to produce rope and twine, in particular 'flax of a suitable growth for the maritime climate of Rhode Island'. This was fulfilled by sending selections of seed from the flax and hemp fields around Bridport which was the mainstay of the British net-making industry.

Reinforcing his propaganda campaign in England on behalf of the settlers, White published a *Planters' Plea* in 1630. Here the words 'plant' and 'plantation' were used in their Ulster context, in terms of emigration and settlement, rather than in a botanical or woodland sense.

Strains and struggles led to allegations of financial impropriety being made against White in 1635. He was examined by Sir John Lambe in respect of moneys that had been sent to Dr John Stoughton in New England. The scandal disrupted White's life for six months but was eventually dismissed as being merely 'twattling' gossip. Considerable sums had been sent, it was established, but these had been legally raised and rightfully paid. The most substantial single contribution came as a legacy from Philippa Pitt. She had bequeathed the money to White but intended him to accept it on behalf of the Massachusetts Bay colonists.

A decade later, White became embroiled in the turmoil of the English Civil War. John White's House, behind Dorset County Museum and St Peter's Church in the middle of Dorchester, was ravaged by Royalists of Prince Rupert's regiment. His possessions were looted and books destroyed. During Oliver Cromwell's puritan regime, White was back in favour and a figure of influence in Westminster. He was offered a prestigious position as warden of New College, Oxford. It was too late, he replied, as he was now 'sick and infirm, a dying man'.

John White died on 21 July 1648. He was buried in St Peter's Church, High West Street, Dorchester, where the state flag of Massachusetts now hangs above the pulpit. His inscription reads:

'In this porch lies the body of Revd John White M.A. of New College, Oxford. He was born at Christmas 1575. For about 40 years he was rector of this parish and also of Holy Trinity, Dorchester. He died here 21st July 1648. A man of great godliness, good scholarship and wonderful ability and kindness, He had a very strong sway in this town. He greatly set forward the emigration to the Massachusetts Bay Colony where his name lives in unfading remembrance.'

Those early Dorset settlers also brought Wareham and Weymouth as placenames to Massachusetts. As the Province of Massachusetts Bay, this became the first region in the American colonies to declare independence, after its assembly had been dissolved by Governor Gage. A provincial congress met there at Concord in October 1774, under the presidency of John Hancock, and proclaimed the right to raise taxes as well as responsibility for protecting public safety.

Dorset-born Joseph Bucklin, from Rhode Island, faced the British redcoats at Concord on the day that went into history. It was he who stood in the line of 'embattled farmers' and in the words of essayist and poet Ralph Waldo Emerson, 'fired the shot heard round the world'. After the American Revolution, the assembly in Massachusetts abolished slavery in 1783, and declared its statehood by adopting the Constitution of the United States in 1788.

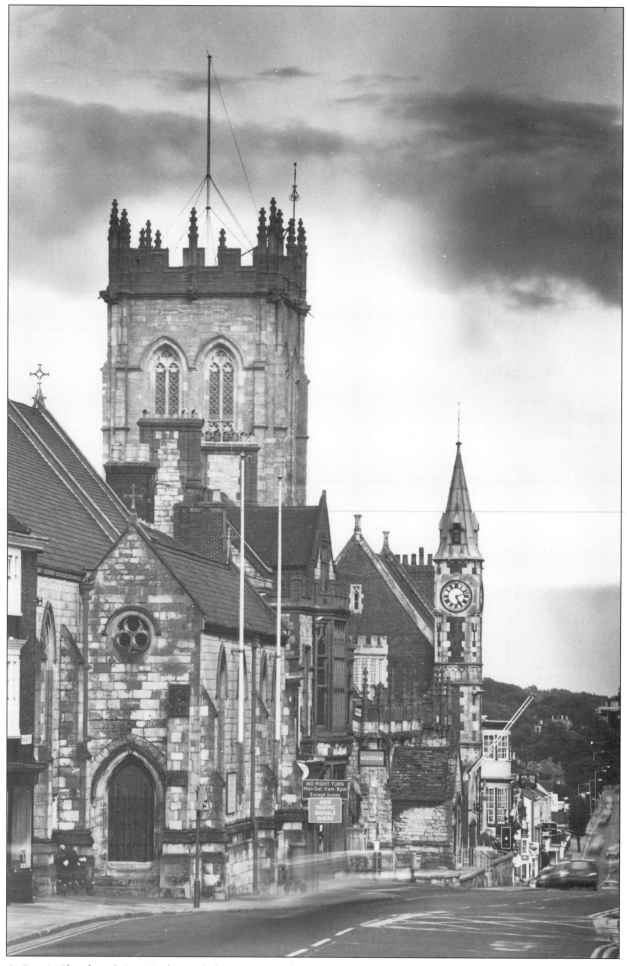

St Peter's Church and Corn Exchange, looking down High West Street, in Dorchester.

Judicial arrivals, for prayers to open an Assize court, through the porch commemorating Revd John White at St Peter's Church in the 1960s.

EAST CHALDON

Elizabeth and Hope Muntz

St Nicholas's Church – SY 790 831

The mediaevalist Isabelle Hope Muntz (1907–81) and her sister Elizabeth Muntz (1894–1977), the sculptor, are buried in the churchyard at East Chaldon, beside Chaldon Herring parish church. Both were born in Toronto, Canada, to Rupert Gustavus Muntz and his second wife, Lucy Elsie Muntz.

The sisters were highly practical. On leaving private schools in Bournemouth and Eastbourne, Hope Muntz designed aircraft components and specialised in precision-engineering, took up driving with enthusiasm, and threw her energies into Air Raid Precautions. The driving together with riding, combined with an urge to travel, provided material for freelance journalism.

Hope Muntz, who never married, then researched for years to gather the Dorset-based material which she presented in an epic of saga-style perfection, *The Golden Warrior*, which was published in 1948 and translated into German and Scandinavian editions. She also reviewed books, under the pseudonym William Langland, and became the leading British scholar of the Battle of Hastings and its Bayeux Tapestry depiction.

This material and its artistry inspired her elder sister, Elizabeth, who produced the primitive nativity painting for the church at East Chaldon which has the barrow-studded skyline escarpment of the Five Marys, overlooking the village, as its backdrop. Elizabeth also cut the grave-slab for author Llewelyn Powys which is set beside the upper of the parish's two coastal footpaths that look down on Weymouth Bay.

Llewelyn Powys

No. 5, Coastguard Cottages, White Nothe – SY 772 809

Llewelyn Powys (1884–1939), like his elder brother John Cowper Powys (1872–1963), made numerous extended trips to New York where he lectured and wrote newspaper articles. There, in 1921, he met a 'delicately ironic hostess, whose round white arms seemed to me then, as I looked at them in the flickering light of the canal-coal fire, as delectable as dairy junket, and whose fair hair worn so as to conceal as far as possible the prominence of an over-high forehead, was of a fairer and more fine texture than ever was the hair of that lovely chatelaine who so long ago would sit beneath the glittering holly trees of Brittany'. She was Alyse Gregory – the editor of *The Dial*. They married and sailed from Brooklyn for England in 1925. 'It's disgraceful of me to have persuaded Alyse to give up

The Dial,' he wrote to his sister Gertrude, 'But I want to come home.' They took No.5 Coastguard Cottages, near the hamlet of East Chaldon.

Alyse and 'Lulu' Powys shared friendships with Louis Umfreville Wilkinson (1881–1966), Arnold Bennett (1867–1931), Dorothy Cheston and Julian Huxley (1887–1975). Wilkinson and the writer Ann Reid spent the Christmas of 1925 with them at No. 5, Coastguard Cottages, on the summit of White Nothe headland (which Powys insisted on calling White Nose, for its snout-like profile). It stands between Ringstead Bay and the downlands of East Chaldon, at 548 feet above sea level, with the highest buildings on the Dorset coast. Visitors were sometimes less than impressed, Llewelyn wrote to Reginald Marsh, giving the example of lecturer Louis Wilkinson who retired to Dove Cottage at Hazelbury Bryan in Dorset and wrote as Louis Marlow. The problem was that he 'did not like the wine'.

Llewelyn, fighting kidney disease and tuberculosis, was a natural rebel against rich living. Even that cannot excuse his confession that he was unable to tell the difference between freshly-opened choice Burgundy and dreggs of the same in an oxidised state a week later. All the visitors seemed to bring their problems. Naomi Mitchison rode on a dog-cart from Wool station and arrived in a gale. She anguished over an unflattering review of her first book in the *New York Herald-Tribune* only to find that Llewelyn had written it.

Worse befell Walter Franzen, visiting from the United States, who set off alone towards the famous rock-arch at Durdle Door where he was going to bathe. He had three hours in which to do so, being due to return for lunch at one o'clock, but was never seen alive again.

His body was later found on the beach – directly below Bat's Head – midway between White Nothe and Durdle Door. He had either jumped or fallen from the cliff directly above and his watch had stopped at 12.45. Although the act could have been deliberate, he might simply have slipped while running the last couple of miles to return to the cottage, along the smooth dry turf of a hazardous seaward-sloping clifftop.

Revd Hamilton Johnson, Llewelyn's cousin, was next on the guest list and arrived at the cottage the day after the tragedy. He carried out the task of burying Walter Franzen in East Chaldon churchyard.

Alyse and Llewelyn sailed back to New York for Christmas in 1927. Ford Madox Ford went off with Llewelyn's walking stick on Christmas Eve. Back at White Nothe, via the Holy Land and Rome, Alyse Gregory received good news on 10 May 1930. Her manuscript *King Log and Lady Lea* was accepted for publication. Llewelyn had finished *The Cradle of God* as *Fables* which appeared as a limited edition and he started work on *The Pathetic Fallacy*. Wine connoisseur Louis Wilkinson celebrated the appearance of his novel *Mr Amberthwaite* and stayed with Ann Reid in an adjoining cottage. This time he brought his own bottles. Rivers Pollock was another visitor.

Returning from an extended visit to the United States and the West Indies, in 1931, Alyse Gregory and Llewelyn Powys found that Louis Wilkinson and Ann Reid had moved into Chydyok. As a result they also decided to share a remote farmhouse, Chydyok Farm, in its own dry valley a mile south of East Chaldon, with his sisters Gertrude and Katie Powys. Ann Reid, a novelist with *We are Dead* and *Love Lies Bleeding*, died suddenly at Watchet, Somerset, in January 1931.

The book illustrator Robert Gibbings (1889–1958) became a frequent visitor and Llewelyn's favourite walk was south-eastwards, to Lulworth Cove, where they could have lunch. When walking alone, however, he headed for the coastal viewpoint of Fountain Rock, memorably during the intense heat of 1933.

'I walk naked over the hills delighting in the summer sunshine,' he wrote to brother John. In *Love and Death* he celebrated what had become 'the happiest summer of my life':

'How exultantly I honoured the Sun that summer, god of triumphant life, rising in his giant's strength morning after morning.'

The book was originally entitled *Life and Death*. John Cowper Powys moved into Rats Barn at East Chaldon and helped look after both Llewelyn and Alyse during bouts of his haemorrhaging and her neuralgia. Llewelyn wrote to the White House to express concern at the rise of Hitler and received a personal reply from President Roosevelt in 1934.

His next political intervention brought Llewelyn to court. Having protested about child abuse at a local home for mentally defective girls, he found himself in the dock in Dorchester accused of criminal libel, along with West Chaldon farmer James Cobb and lesbian authors Sylvia Townsend Warner and Valentine Ackland. Each was fined £100 plus costs. Llewelyn had to be carried down the valley from Chydeock 'like some buggerly Buddha for the populace to bawl at and the seagulls to molest'. He met Mrs Florence Hardy, the widow of novelist Thomas, with her driver on the village green. Llewelyn insisted on paying all the fines but James Cobb declined the offer. Llewelyn replied:

'God! You are of the true old stock, such as are not often to be found now-a-days and if there were more Christians like you I would soon feel like respecting them.'

National newspapers gave Llewelyn the headlines on placards and front-pages. 'Dying Man in Dorset Assize Drama,' they proclaimed. 'Verdict of Malice against Dying Author.' Friends such as Arthur Ficke and Rivers Pollock came to his aid in paying the damages. As for his health, it was his brother Bertie Powys of the Society for the Protection of Ancient Buildings who pre-deceased him in March 1936. Llewelyn continued writing his essays and travelled to Switzerland. *Ebony and Ivory* was revised for a sixpenny paperback edition in the Penguin list. Llewelyn, who had been living for the moment for years, knew he had little time left:

'To be alive, only to be alive, may I never forget the privilege of that.'

He lasted out, however, until the first winter of the Second World War and died in Clavadel on 2 December 1939 which was the third anniversary of his final departure from England. His ashes were returned after the years of conflict. The urn was buried beneath a slab of Portland stone, carved by the Canadian-born sculptor Elizabeth Muntz, overlooking his favourite view of Weymouth Bay from the coastal slope between Fountain Rock and Chydyok.

The essayist Llewelyn Powys split his life between New York and Dorset.

Above: *White Nothe Cottages, at 548 feet above sea level, are the highest buildings on the Dorset coast.*

Right: *Chalk cliffs between Durdle Door and White Nothe* (top) *from which one of Powys's American visitors fell to his death.*

Chydyok Farm, between East Chaldon and the sea, was Llewelyn Powys's last home.

'The living, the living, he shall praise thee' is the epitaph to Llewelyn Powys (1884–1939) on his cliffside grave.

HAMWORTHY

RMS *Mauretania*

The Boat House, 75 Lake Drive — SY 985 903

Overlooking the Wareham Channel with views across Poole Harbour to Arne peninsula and the Purbeck Hills, the Boat House is a remarkable building dating from 1935. It was constructed around the lavish panelling of the captain's quarters and three cabins of the 31,938-ton RMS *Mauretania*. She was built in Scotland, at Swan Hunter's shipyard, and launched into the River Clyde on 20 September 1906. Her maiden voyage was from Liverpool on 16 November 1907. Fame followed fast as she held and defended the prestigious Blue Riband for the fastest transatlantic crossing.

Then the sedate luxury liner of the Cunard fleet became known as 'The Grand Old Lady of the Atlantic'. By this time the French had taken the Blue Riband. She sailed for the last time to New York on 26 September 1934, on the very day that her successor the *Queen Mary* was launched in Glasgow, into the Clyde. History had moved on.

The *Mauretania* was withdrawn from service and sold for scrap in April 1935. First she was stripped of her fittings from which the Boat House received the best pickings. The Boat House, at No. 75 Lake Drive, Hamworthy, is a mass of luxury fittings, furnishings and port-holes, though it also had normal picture windows. Maple-wood from the drawing room of a predecessor, the first great ship to be named *Mauretania*, is enriched with gilt-carved sea urchins, leaf courses, dishes and pans, and ornamental hanging wreaths. Inserted into these panels are numerous mirrors as well as cupboards for books and china.

Flowing art-deco settee frames, with leaf-carved cresting rails and panelled ends, adorn the corners of the ground floor lounge. This is 30 feet by 22 feet and has the panoramic views. The first owner of the Boat House was London businessman Tom Cullen who used it as a weekend retreat. His son, Peter Cullen, often came with him, as did colleagues and friends. The Hatchard family provided their staff and shared the building from the winter of 1935 through to 1951, apart from wartime breaks due to invasion fears, bombs and the preparations for D-Day.

The captain's cabin from the liner Mauretania, *around which the Boat House was built at Hamworthy, in 1935.*

The gallery forming the centrepiece to the Boat House.

The newly-constructed Boat House at Lake Drive, Hamworthy, concealing its transatlantic interior.

Tribute stamp to RMS Mauretania – 'the Grand Old Lady of the Atlantic'.

HURN

Post-war transatlantic flights

Bournemouth International Airport – SZ 110 980

Late in 1944 wartime RAF Hurn, in the Stour meadows north of Bournemouth, became the main landplane base for British Overseas Airways Corporation, as distinct from its international flying-boat services which came and went from the 'sea aero-drome' in nearby Poole Harbour. Dakotas on European and Middle East services flew from Whitchurch near Bristol. The manager of operations from Hurn was Captain J. C. Harrington.

The BOAC navigation branch's 'World Map for the Air Age' showed straight lines centred on London. The reality was somewhat different. Hurn was actually at its hub. Staff for the national airline complained that they had been 'pitchforked into the place' which had been left as 'an unholy shambles'. They had to carry out 'open-air maintenance' or retreat to 'unheated hangars'. Only three of these were wide enough to take Lancastrians, Liberators, or Yorks.

From 15 July 1945 the Avro Lancastrians on the Australian route clipped the flight time from seventy-two hours to sixty-three hours. Refuelling stops were at Lydda, in British-controlled Palestine, and Karachi in British India. Here the BOAC crews swapped places with their Quantas counterparts for the remainder of the flight to Sydney. Karachi had its own direct service from England, operated by Avro York transports, from 16 July 1945. The journey took thirty-one hours (cutting two hours from the previous time achieved by flying-boats and land-planes).

The double declarations of surrender in 1945, between and after VE Day and VJ Day, were followed by a massive expansion of civilian services. These were initially restricted to 'very important persons' and others of lesser standing who met the stringent qualifications. They had to show a military or strategic need to travel in haste in the national cause. Following the re-establishment of the peace those with money could also buy a passage.

Europe's other beleaguered colonial powers also operated international flights from Hurn. The most frequent was Sabena's service to Leopoldville in the Belgian Congo which continued through 1944 and the first half of 1945 until its transfer to Evere Airport, Brussels. The final outgoing flight from Hurn was scheduled for 25 July 1945. The last incoming arrival touched down at Hurn on 5 August 1945 and then lifted off for Brussels.

On 16 September 1945, an ex-military C-54 Skymaster of Pan American Airways landed at Hurn from La Guardia, New York, after a seventeen-hour proving flight via Gander in Newfoundland. In October 1945, the first of a fleet of Avro Yorks from Hurn landed in Pretoria after sixty-eight hours sixteen minutes, to establish the Britain-South Africa run. The weekly 'Springbok Service' to Johannesburg, shared with South African Airways, was inaugurated with the arrival of a York at Hurn on 12 November 1945.

There was also a thrice-weekly freight and post service in Halifax VIIIC transports from Hurn to Accra via Rabat and Bathurst. The trip involved twenty-three flying hours at an average speed of 200 miles per hour.

By November 1945 the 'Where You Can Fly From Here' leaflet listed eight regular routes from Hurn which spanned the globe:

'1. Castel Benito – Cairo – Khartoum – Nairobi – Johannesburg (British Overseas Airways Corporation and South African Airways).
2. Lydda – Karachi – Ceylon – Learmonth – Sydney

(BOAC and Quantas Empire Airways). Connecting services from Sydney to Auckland (Tasman Empire Airways, with a transpacific link being established to Honolulu and Vancouver).

3. Marseilles – Malta – El Adem – Cairo – Lydda – Baghdad – Basra – Sharjah – Karachi (BOAC).

4. Malta – Cairo – Basra – Karachi (BOAC, extended to Calcutta).

5. Lisbon – Rabat – Port Etienne – Bathurst – Freetown – Takoradi – Accra (BOAC, extended to Lagos – Kano – Maiduguri – El Geneina – El Fasher – Khartoum – Wadi Halfa – Luxor – Cairo).

6. Lisbon – Gibraltar (Koninklijke Luchtvaart Maatschappij for BOAC).

7. Lisbon – Azores – Bermuda – New York (Pan American Airways).

8. Rineanna – Gander – Boston – New York (American Overseas Airways).'

The American airlines flew Lockheed Constellations. Newly-arrived converted Halifax Mark VIII C-version transports, with four Bristol Hercules engines, were also based at Hurn. The pannier below its fuselage carried up to 8000 pounds of freight. BOAC set about establishing a pattern of flights every other day to the French colony of Algiers, and then across the Sahara to Kano in British northern Nigeria, then westwards to colonial Accra on the Gold Coast. Colonial officials and their families would be the major clientele.

Current offerings from Bournemouth International Airport include occasional trans-Atlantic crossings – such as Palmiar to Orlando – and the return of a vintage wartime Dakota, the principal American and European transport of the conflict and post-war world. This made half-hour pleasure flights and longer cross-Channel excursions over the French beaches and battlefields. As RAF Hurn, the airport had seen extensive use by the United States Army Air Force, in preparation for D-Day and the subsequent Battle of Normandy.

American visitors to Hurn Aerodrome from 31 October to the night of 3-4 November 1942 were headed by Brigadier-General Jimmy Doolittle (left) and Lieutenant-General Dwight D. Eisenhower.

Planned at Hurn, with take-off in Flying Fortresses for Gibraltar, Generals Eisenhower and Doolittle landed in Morocco on 8 November 1942.

HURN

Longest-ever flight

Bournemouth International Airport — SZ 110 980

The American adventurer Steve Fossett, having flown solo in a circuit of the earth and almost a quarter of a second circuit, established an all-time record for distance and duration at Bournemouth in February 2006. He secured the record when he flew over Shannon at 15.35 hours Greenwich Mean Time on Saturday 10 February 2006, and was intending to continue to Manston, Kent, but found himself forced to abort the flight from 40,000 feet on suffering an acute fuel shortage coupled with an electrical failure as his generator cut out.

Fossett issued a mayday signal from his specially made ultra light-weight Virgin Atlantic Global Flyer. Air Traffic Control at Swanwick, Southampton, gave him the option of coming into Cardiff or Bournemouth. The sixty-one-year-old aviator had landed before at Bournemouth, which also happens to be closer to Kent.

The crash alarm was activated at Hurn, giving twenty minutes notice of the emergency arrival, with Fossett having just twenty-five minutes reserve electrical power available from his batteries.

In the event, despite the further complication of two blown tyres, the Global Flyer landed safely from the blue sky of a late winter afternoon. British entrepreneur, sponsor and friend Sir Richard Branson – following in an accompanying jet – landed half an hour later to begin the celebrations.

Fossett's epic flight, of eighty hours eastwards with the jet stream from Cape Canaveral, Florida, covered 26,389 miles. It comprised one complete circuit of the northern hemisphere plus 79 degrees of longitude into a second.

IWERNE MINSTER

The Ismays and *Titanic*

Clayesmore School – ST 863 147

When James Hainsworth Ismay (1867–1930) sold the White Star Fleet to American financier J. Pierpoint Morgan, in 1902, it enabled him to purchase an 1880-built Dorset mansion from Lord Wolverton. This was Iwerne Minster House which now houses Clayesmore School. With his second wife, Muriel Harriett Charles Macdonald Moreton, he threw his efforts into establishing a sporting estate.

Ismay was the younger brother of Bruce Ismay, full name Joseph Bruce Ismay (1862–1937) who came to Iwerne Minster House for rest and recreation. He shrugged off his anxieties with motoring, golfing and shooting. From April 1912, for the rest of their lives, the Ismay brothers were inextricably linked with the fateful story of the world's most famous vessel since Noah's Ark.

British steamship number 131,428 was built by Harland and Wolff at Belfast and registered at the port of Liverpool. The 46,328-ton three-screw vessel had four elliptical-shaped funnels, three taking fumes from the 55,000 horsepower coal-burning boilers, and the after-one acting as a ventilator. Fitted out as an ocean-liner, SS *Titanic* sailed from Southampton for New York on her maiden voyage. The route was via Cherbourg in France and Queenstown in southern Ireland. She departed from the latter on 1 April 1912.

She was the thirteenth and most magnificent of the fleet owned by the Ocean Steam Navigation Company which was universally known as the White Star Line. It carried passengers, mails and cargo between Europe and New York. Though all but eight shares were held by the International Navigation Company of Liverpool, part of seventy-five-year-old Pierpoint Morgan's empire, operational control remained with the Ismay family, in the person of Bruce Ismay as

chairman and managing director. Having chosen *Titanic* for her name, as sister-ship to the *Olympic*, Bruce Ismay sailed on the maiden voyage and became the most knowledgeable survivor. He was the prime contributor to Wreck Commissioner Viscount Mersey's official report on the loss of the vessel.

He stated that the masters of vessels belonging to the White Star Line were not given special 'sailing orders' before commencement of a particular voyage. It was understood, however, that they would follow accepted 'tacks' or 'lane routes' as agreed by 'the great steamship companies'. Any deviations had to be reported on and explained at the end of the crossing.

What may not have been left in the sole judgment of the captain was the speed of Titanic's first oceanic voyage. This was approximately 22 knots – 'high speed, though not at the ship's maximum' – when she ploughed along beside an iceberg in almost total darkness. There had been a conversation at Queenstown between Bruce Ismay and the chief engineer, Joseph Bell, about the need for speed and the consequent consumption of coal. This, allegedly, was an improper interference in the matter that caused Captain Edward J. Smith to maintain his course and speed despite an ice-warning.

Lord Mersey discounted the suggestion:

'I do not believe this. The evidence shows that he was not trying to make any record passage or indeed any exceptionally quick passage. He was not trying to please anybody but was exercising his own discretion in the way he thought best. He made a mistake, a very grievous mistake, but one in which he cannot be said to have had any part, and in the absence of negligence it is, in my opinion, impossible to fix Captain Smith with blame. It is, however, to be hoped that the last

has been heard of the practice and that for the future it will be abandoned for what we now know to be more prudent and wiser measures. What was a mistake in the case of the Titanic *would without doubt be negligence in any similar case in the future.'*

Lord Mersey's reference to accepted practice was the fact that 'for a quarter of a century or more' liners had maintained their intended course and speed through ice-strewn seas and trusted 'to a sharp look-out to enable them to avoid the danger'. He felt, with hindsight, that Captain Smith should either have veered 'well to the south' or 'reduced speed materially as night approached. He did neither. The alteration of course at 5.50 pm was so insignificant that it cannot be attributed to any intention to avoid ice. This deviation brought the vessel back to within about 2 miles of the customary route before 11.30 pm. And there was certainly no reduction of speed.'

Bruce Ismay escaped less lightly in the case of culpability in the interception of a wireless message received from the steamship Baltic at 1.42 pm *Titanic* time pm Sunday 14 April. It was the second ice-warning to reach the liner:

'*Captain Smith,* Titanic. *Have had moderate, variable winds and clear, fine weather since leaving. Greek steamer* Athenia *reports passing icebergs and large quantities of field ice today in Latitude 41 degrees 51 minutes north, Longitude 49 degrees 52 minutes west. Last night we spoke* [to the] *German oiltank steamer* Deutschland, [bound from] *Stettin to Philadelphia, not under control. Short of coal. Latitude 40 degrees 42 minutes north, Longitude 55 degrees 11 minutes west. Wishes to be reported to New York and other steamers. Wish you and* Titanic *all success.'*

This was received in the Marconi room and acknowledged by *Titanic* at 42 degrees 33 minutes north, 45 degrees 50 minutes west. Lord Mersey's finding was strongly critical of what happened next:

'*Mr Ismay, the Managing Director of the White Star Line, was on board the* Titanic, *and it appears that the Master handed the* Baltic's *message to Mr Ismay almost immediately after it was received. This no doubt was in order that*

Mr Ismay might know that ice was to be expected. Mr Ismay states that he understood from this message that they would get up to the ice 'that night'. Mr Ismay showed this message to two ladies, and it is therefore possible that many persons on board became aware of its contents. This message ought in my opinion to have been put on the board in the chart-room as soon as it was received. It remained, however, in Mr Ismay's possession until 7.15 pm when the Master asked Mr Ismay to return it. It was then that it was first posted in the chart-room.'*

The first ice-warning had come from Captain James Barr on the steamship *Caronia*. Others came from the *Californian* and Captain Lord on the *Antillian*. The fifth such wireless message in Morse code was as starkly ominous as any warning could be, even without the benefit of hindsight. It came from a steamer of the Atlantic Transport Line:

'*From* Mesaba *to* Titanic *and all west-bound ships. Ice report in Latitude 42 degrees north to 41 degrees 25 minutes north, Longitude 49 degrees to Longitude 50 degrees 30 minutes west. Saw much heavy pack ice and a great number large icebergs. Also field ice. Weather good, clear.'*

The tragedy was that this crucial message, received in the radio room by senior operator Jack Phillips, does not appear to have reached the Master or any of the officers:

'*The Marconi operator was very busy from 8 o'clock onward transmitting messages via Cape Race for passengers on board the* Titanic, *and the probability is that he failed to grasp the significance and importance of the message, and put it aside until he should be less busy. It was never acknowledged by Captain Smith, and I am satisfied that it was never received by him.'*

In fairness to wireless operators Jack Phillips and Harold Bride, their Marconi set had broken down the previous evening, and they were struggling to send a backlog of messages onwards to America.

Once the inevitable had happened, at about 11.40 pm *Titanic* time (9.50 pm New York time) the scraping woke Bruce Ismay in his luxury suite on B Deck. He went up to the bridge to ask Captain Smith if the ship was seriously damaged.

'I'm afraid she is,' he replied.

There was general good order, though slowness among the women to appreciate the seriousness of the situation and take to the lifeboats, but Lord Mersey heard stinging personal criticism of Sir Cosmo Duff Cooper and his friend Bruce Ismay as more than 1500 were losing their lives. The *Titanic* went down at 2.20 am ship's time (12.30 am New York time) on Monday 15 April 1912.

Senator Raynor, speaking in New York, denounced Ismay as 'the officer who was primarily responsible for the disaster who has reached his destination in safety and unharmed'.

Defending himself, Bruce Ismay asked:

'What sort [of person] *do you think I am? Do you believe I'm the sort that would have left the ship as long as there were any women or children on board her? That is the thing that hurts, and hurts all the more because it is so false and baseless.'*

Lord Mersey exonerated both Sir Cosmo Duff Cooper and Bruce Ismay:

'As to the attack on Mr Bruce Ismay, it resolved itself into the suggestion that, occupying the position of the Managing Director of the Steamship Company, some moral duty was imposed upon him to wait on board until the vessel foundered. I do not agree. Mr Ismay, after rendering assistance to many passengers, found 'C' collapsible, the last boat on the starboard side, actually being lowered. No other people were there at the time. There was room for him and he jumped in. Had he not jumped he would merely have added one more life, namely, his own, to the number of those lost.'

Of the 1316 passengers, and 885 crew, a total of 2201 on board, there were 711 survivors. Only one in three were saved overall, rising to two in three for 1st Class passengers. The crew suffered the worst toll; less than one in four survived, due to the fact that 'for the most part all attended to their duties to the last, and until all the boats were gone'.

Bodies littered the sea. A total of about 320 were recovered. The James Dawson lying among 122 Titanic victims at Fairview cemetery in Windsor Road, Halifax, Nova Scotia, is not quite the Jack Dawson of Leonardo DiCaprio's character in James Cameron's blockbuster movie. Not that it spares him a succession of girlie tributes. The real James Dawson was a Dublin-born coal trimmer, among the 3rd Class Irish emigrants who boarded at Queenstown. He probably lacked the youthful looks of Jack in the film and certainly never received 1st Class hospitality.

Brue Ismay erected a much more elaborate memorial to his secretary and confidant Ernest Edward Samuel Freeman. Most poignant of the Halifax graves is the stone to the 'Unknown Child' – a blond two-year-old boy – that was erected by the crew of the cable-laying ship *Mackay-Bennett* who accomplished the gruesome task of collecting more than 300 of the recovered bodies.

The rest, as they say, is cinema.

Artist's impression of SS Titanic *under-way on her fateful maiden voyage.*

Above: *Iwerne Minster House, now Clayesmore School, at the heart of the Ismay family's shooting estate.*

Left: *Bruce Ismay, managing director of the White Star Line, survived the loss of SS* Titanic *but his integrity and reputation were destroyed.*

Below: *Commemorative cards for the loss of the liner* Titanic *on her maiden voyage across the Atlantic in April 1912.*

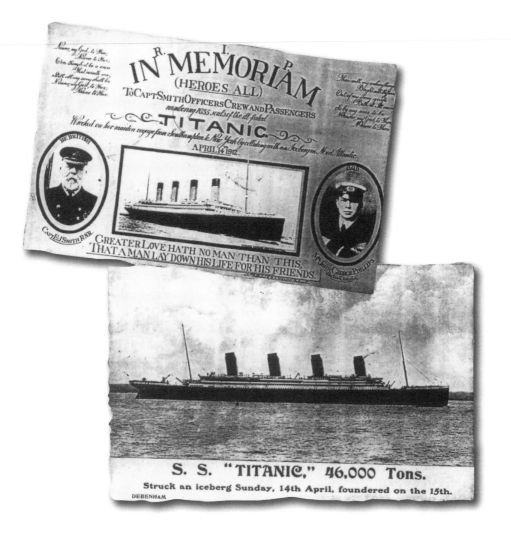

KINGSTON RUSSELL

John Lothrop Motley

Kingston Russell House – SY 573 895

John Lothrop Motley (1814–77), eminent historian of the Dutch Republic and United States envoy extraordinary and Minister Plenipotentiary to the Court of St James in London, was born in Dorchester, New England, and died near Dorchester, in old England. Whilst on vacation, he realised his health was weakening and though not suffering an obvious illness told his companions: 'It has come, it has come.'

He was elected posthumously to the American Hall of Fame, but he already had an English memorial stone in the doorway of the house where he died, with an inscription by its owner, the Duke of Bedford:

'John Lothrop Motley, Minister of the United States, Historian of the Dutch Republic, died at Kingston Russell House, 29th May, 1877.'

Motley had been visiting his daughter, Mrs Sheridan, at Frampton Court, near Maiden Newton. He was a career diplomat, as secretary of the United States legation in St Petersburg in 1841 and the ambassador to Austria from 1861 to 1867, and then the UK in 1869–70. Since 1847 he had been studying the history of the Netherlands and publication of *The Rise of the Dutch Republic*, in 1856, was followed by *The History of the United Netherlands* in two volumes, 1860–61, and *The Life and Death of John Barneveld* in 1874.

The classical lines of Kingston Russell House stand in the Bride Valley to the south of the A35 road 7 miles west of Dorchester. Motley's London home was at 17 Arlington Street and he is buried beside his wife in the big municipal cemetery at Kensal Green. His election to the American Hall of Fame followed in 1910.

LULWORTH

Hercules crash

off Lulworth Cove – SY 825 797

An advanced radar drama exploded off the Purbeck coast in May 1969, though what happened is still partly supposition, for papers released in the United States through the Freedom of Information Act have been heavily censored. The case, at the height of the Cold War, concerns a dramatic instance of the occasional tradition throughout the American Forces for suicidal misappropriation of military hardware.

An Assistance Crew Chief, Sergeant Paul Adams Meyer of the 36th Tactical Air Service, United States Air Force, had stolen a 30-ton Lockheed C-130E Hercules transporter – one of the last generation of heavy military turbo-props, carrying advanced electronics – from RAF Mildenhall airbase in East Anglia. It belonged to the 513th Tactical Air wing of the 3rd Air Force, USAFE (United States Air Force, Europe).

Psychologically, Paul Meyer had a problem, it soon emerges from the 'USAF Accident / Incident Report'. Privacy considerations prevent us knowing the detail, but it seems he married eight weeks earlier in Poquoson, Virginia, before being sent from Langley Air Force Base to Britain. He had been passed over for promotion but there was also a personal difficulty, concerning which he 'verbally requested to be returned to Langley AFB to aid his wife in settling the problem'.

On Thursday 22 May 1969, Sergeant Meyer:

'...performed his normal duties as assistant crew chief on C-130, SN (serial number) 37789, by accompanying the aircraft on a one day flight to Germany. Upon return to RAF Mildenhall he was invited by Sergeant Carpenter to a house party in a nearby town. Sgt. Carpenter loaned Sgt. Meyer a pair of civilian trousers and Sgt. Meyer changed out of his flight clothes at Sgt. Carpenter's barracks. The two

sergeants, in company with five other companions, proceeded to the party in taxis at 19.00 CET (Central European Time; following sentence CENSORED). However, during the later hours he was (word CENSORED) drinking rather heavily, and behaving erratically. He left the house on three or four occasions going into the garden and generally causing a disturbance.'

His friends tried to console him but he was last seen 'crossing a rooftop' and the next they heard he had been arrested by civilian police 'and charged with being drunk and disorderly'. His mood was changeable: 'At times he was co-operative and then would suddenly become sarcastic and belligerent.' The police released him into military custody, during which he attempted to escape through a latrine window, and was eventually returned to his billet after being told he 'was restricted to barracks and was grounded'.

He appeared to be preparing for bed but instead slipped out and stole the vehicle keys of Captain Upton, the 36th Tactical Air Service Materiel Officer. Using the assumed name 'Captain Epstein' he requested fuel for Hercules 37789, on hardstand 21:

'The POL dispatcher thought it unusual that a captain was requesting fuel, however, it had happened to him before so he honored the request.' Suspicions were not otherwise aroused despite his physical presence, as Sgt. Meyer had frequently been on the flight line between 02.00-06.00 using the aircraft high frequency radios to talk to his wife by phone patch through the Tactical Air Command Post at Langley Air Force Base. Also, he had on many occasions shown up two to three hours early on days that his aircraft was scheduled to fly. Since the schedule was not until 10.30 Central European Time, Sgt. Johnson saw no reason to contact Operations, at that early hour, concerning a possible mission change. (Next words CENSORED) *missions are frequently changed at the last minute.* (Following sentence and the entirety of the next three paragraphs CENSORED.)

'Upon completion of the fuelling operation, aircraft 37789 contained approximately 60,000 pounds of fuel. (Remainder of paragraph CENSORED, as are crucial parts of the preparation for take-off.) *As he approached the front of 37789 one of the crew chiefs in the truck noticed that chocks had been removed. Staff Sergeant Alexander stopped at Maintenance Control and was informed by* (name CENSORED) *that Sgt. Meyer was at his aircraft. Staff Sgt. Alexander decided to check on Sgt. Meyer after delivering the other two crew chiefs to their aircraft.* (Sentence CENSORED.)

'As he approached the front of 37789 one of the crew chiefs in the truck noticed that the chocks had been removed. Staff Sgt. Alexander stopped his vehicle in front of the aircraft and saw Sgt. Meyer in the pilot's seat. Sgt. Meyer motioned violently for Staff Sgt. Alexander to get out of the way, flashed his taxi lights several times, and moved the throttles into the flight range, near maximum power. Upon observing these actions, considering the safety of the vehicle occupants and not realising the intent for flight, Staff Sgt. Alexander immediately moved his vehicle away from the front of the aircraft. Sgt. Meyer released the brakes and taxied from the hardstand.'

He took a minute and a half to proceed 'from the beginning of the taxi' at 05.06 European Standard Time, through to 'beginning of takeoff roll'. People were now in panic around the edge of the base, with Staff Sergeant Johnson telling the Law Enforcement Desk Sergeant: 'We have a crew chief taxiing an airplane. Stop him.'

They almost did, with two patrol vehicles:

'The amazingly fast reaction of the Security Police patrols was voided due to the lack of an established and practised procedure on just how to stop an aircraft. Also, confirmation that they had the right aircraft was not received in time nor could the one patrol get permission to use his weapon.

'Sgt. Meyer continued his takeoff roll and made (few words CENSORED) *a short field takeoff at 05.08 - 05.10*

Central European Time. He left the ground in an extreme wing low attitude and began an immediate left turn.'

Radar units at both Mildenhall and Lakenheath 'tracked the erratic flight path' until the aircraft was about 50 miles south. Meyer flew the plane single-handed into the busiest air lanes in the world, and then vanished, according to contemporary reports. The American investigation found that 'contact was not established again until twenty minutes later, by Southern Radar located near London'.

Defence and ground-control radar systems had failed to follow the movements of one of the largest and slowest military aircraft. The *Daily Express* reported that the Hercules 'made a hole in Britain's delicate radar system' – for the technically bizarre reason that 'the plane was going out, not coming in'. Three weeks later there was a statement in Parliament that the plane had been 'continuously tracked by British radar'.

The fact was that Paul Meyer flew over the River Thames and across Kent on automatic pilot, with Mildenhall's control centre only able to register his position when Meyer spoke on his radio. He was using his tried and tested technique to get through to his wife in Virginia. Some claimed that Hercules 37789 was invisible to radar as it carried the latest package of electronics for absorbing radar waves and preventing them from being reflected back to the ground.

By turning right, westwards down the entire length of the English Channel, he minimised the chance of ploughing into a built-up area and also lessened the chances of mid-air collision. As he flew off the Lizard he hooked up to his wife via the radio network. She, in a desperate early morning call, tried to talk him into flying the plane back to a British airfield. Mayer's conversation 'was not monitored or recorded' but he obviously intended flying home across the Atlantic Ocean, having requisitioned enough fuel for a full range in excess of 5000 miles. He seems to have been talked out of it.

Meyer carried out a U-turn over the Scilly Isles and crossed Cornwall and south Devon to Lyme Bay. An American F-100 was scrambled from RAF Lakenheath, and a C-130 from Mildenhall, in an effort to assist

Sergeant Meyer by escorting him back to base. Neither established either visual or radar contact. There was anxiety on the ground about the risk of disaster that would inevitably accompany an attempted landing. While an officer who knows the equipment can fly a Hercules without that much difficulty, it is another matter to put the thing back on the ground.

The accident investigation does not mention any direct radio contact between Meyer and Mildenhall. Had it been achieved, and smooth-talking developed into a rapport, the runaway Assistant Crew Chief would have been asked to locate various knobs and panels, as a dry-run of landing techniques. One unconfirmed account of such contact having been established states that in the process he may have touched a red lever the purpose of which he was unaware. This report claims it was the 'destructor', though his superiors would

hardly have called it that over the radio, if they had eventually succeeded in making contact. Anyway, the story of the runaway Hercules ended about 40 miles south of Lulworth Cove, at 06.55 Central European Time on Friday 23 May 1969. Paul Mayer and his plane blew up at co-ordinates 50.00 north (latitude), 02.05 west (longitude).

Western security could relax. There was even a convenient explanation for those at Mildenhall – to suggest Meyer had simply tried to ditch in the sea. Said a spokesman: 'It takes a highly trained and skilled pilot to land on the sea. There's a strong possibility the plane broke up.'

Wreckage was found over the next few days: 'Sgt. Meyer is still missing and presumed dead of injuries sustained when the aircraft impacted the water.'

Lockheed Hercules C130 with advanced electronics, similar to that which crashed off Lulworth, with this being RAF airframe 220 passing low level across Dorset.

LYME REGIS

Thomas Coram

Coram Court and Tower – ST 336 921

Coram Court and Coram Tower, both of which stand opposite and overlooking the big car-park in Pound Road, Lyme Regis, commemorate Thomas Coram (1668–1751) who was born in the town. He emigrated to the United States and made his fortune as a shipbuilder at Taunton in Massachusetts between 1693 and 1704. Together with James Edward Oglethorpe (1696–1785), a British Member of Parliament, he played a leading role in founding the colony of Georgia.

Horace Walpole, in 1735, credited Coram with having unparalleled knowledge about the transatlantic colonies, being 'the honestest, most disinterested, most knowing person about the plantations he had every talked with'.

Both Coram and Oglethorpe were renowned philanthropists. Coram returned to London in 1720 and after seventeen years of fund raising established the Foundling Hospital in Hatton Garden, which was granted a royal charter in 1739, and survives as the Thomas Coram Foundation. A considerable area of land had been acquired, for £7000, with Lord Salisbury donating £500 and insisting that his ground 'as far as Grey's Inn Lane' should also be taken for the project. Hogarth presented a painting and Handel gave concert performances. Once the London charity was safeguarded, Coram abandoned his personal affairs and slid into poverty, putting his final efforts into encouraging friends to provide for the schooling of Indian girls in the American colonies.

Above: *Saint George slaying the dragon, in an 1889-dated carving between Coram Court and Coram Tower, in the shipbuilder's home-town.*

Left: *Mezzotint of William Hogarth's portrait of philanthropist Thomas Coram displayed in the Philpot Museum, Lyme Regis.*

LYTCHETT MINSTER

Flying Fortress crash

Baker's Arms – SY 954 927

An American B-17 bomber, returning from a cross-Channel mission, crashed in fields opposite the thatched roofed Baker's Arms public house, on 2 April 1942. It was a successful emergency landing, ending with the crew congratulating the pilot on his skill in not only bringing them down in one piece, but doing so beside the open doors of a watering hole.

The aircraft had been attempting an approach towards the newly built aerodrome of RAF Hurn, 9 miles to the north-east, but had lost too much height. There was considerable local commotion as people heard or spotted the B-17's descent. David Pearce, aged nine at the time, recalled:

'I was with a group of boys standing on the pillbox beside the railway bridge at Sterte. We saw the plane getting lower

and lower and it came down on Tatchell's Holding at Charity Farm.'

More shocked, literally so, was Mrs Joan Hooper who was in the final stages of pregnancy at Tatchell's Holding, and there were fears of complications. The excitement induced the birth of a healthy baby, with Wendy Hooper being delivered by midwife Margaret Gibson the following day, on Friday 3 April 1942.

By this time Americans were arriving in force, with the earth-moving equipment of an Engineer unit, which based itself at the Baker's Arms and proceeded to remove hedges and flatten three fields into a runway. Another team carried out minor repairs and checks on the B-17, which was then refuelled, and made a smooth take-off for its home base in East Anglia.

MINTERNE MAGNA

Pamela Digby Churchill Hayward Harriman

Minterne House - ST 660 042

The gardens at Minterne House provide the setting for a big Edwardian house as the focal point of the chalkland parish of Minterne Magna, and comprise the visual accompaniment to an historical romance of special significance for American visitors. This is the home of Lord Digby, the 12th Baron Digby in the Irish line, created in 1620, and 5th Baron Digby in the English succession, created 1765. What strikes you with portraits of the Digby family, like those of the Pagets at Plas Newydd, Anglesey, is that the same features recurr, producing dead-ringers across the centuries.

The same applies, in character, to their adventurous women folk. Nineteenth-century Jane Digby became the 'infamous' Lady Ellenborough who went through four husbands, culminating in nearly thirty years of married bliss with Bedouin chief Sheikh Medjuel el Mazrab in Damascus, where she acted as arbitrator between Christians and Arabs.

In the twentieth century her counterpart was the present Lord Digby's sister, Pamela Digby Churchill Hayward Harriman (1920–97), who achieved three celebrity husbands and died in Paris as American Ambassador to France, having collapsed into a coma with a brain haemorrhage, after her daily swim in the Ritz Hotel pool on 5 February 1997. Her body was returned to Washington, arriving in a heavy snowfall the following weekend, when it was lifted off an Air Force jet and carried by a military guard of honour. The Secretary of State, Madeleine Albright, paid the first tribute at Andrews air force base:

'Today we are here to welcome home a great American. She served her country with skill, grace, eloquence and elegance.'

President Bill Clinton had already described her as 'one of the most unusual and gifted people I have ever met'

and went on to deliver the eulogy for her burial at Arden House, New York State. He had sent her to Paris in 1993. The back story, he explained, started off with this English society girl becoming the daughter-in-law of Sir Winston Churchill. Then via an equally newsworthy number of other twists and turns she took up American citizenship, in 1971, and became the doyenne of the Democratic Party.

Those roots began in the Minterne Magna seat of the aristocratic Digby family. War leader Winston Spencer Churchill, then First Lord of the Admiralty, came here after a visit to Portland naval base in October 1939. His son, Randolph Churchill, was marrying Lord Digby's daughter Pamela, and they were already one family as all the Churchills and all the Spencers were descended from George Digby, Earl of Bristol.

The old Minterne House, replaced in 1902–05, had been an historic seat of the Churchill family. The house is not open to the public but can be viewed at close quarters, dominating graceful gardens and lakeland cascades, at the northern end of the Cerne Valley.

Pamela's father never realised what was driving her eventful life, during the war, and was quoted as having naively told a friend:

'Pam's a splendid gel, and she's turned out such a good manager. I only give her a small allowance and the War Office certainly don't pay her much; but, do you know, she's got a flat in Berkeley Square.'

After Randolph Churchill, Pamela married Leland Hayward, and then United States diplomat and railroad heir Averell Harriman. She took all their names to become the Honourable Mrs Pamela Digby

Churchill Hayward Harriman, and Averell's profession as United States Ambassador to Paris.

Much has been written about Pamela Digby's life and liaisons, notably in Christopher Ogden's *Life of the Party* which if it had come out any earlier than 1994 would have blocked her passage, through Senate hearings, to the appointment in Paris. Pamela, according to biographer Sally Bedell Smith, failed after lengthy litigation to secure more than an estimated £5.6 million of Averell Harriman's real estate, but owned a majority interest in the Van Gogh painting 'White Roses'.

Pamela Digby's marriage to Randolph Churchill, son of the First Lord of the Admiralty, was the social event of 1939.

Minterne House, the family home of the Honourable Mrs Pamela Digby Churchill Hayward Harriman, who became United States Ambassador to Paris.

MORETON

Prince Clarence of the Mosquitoes

St Nicholas's Church — SY 806 893

The young Prince Clarence (1835–49), second son of the King of Mosquitoes, died whilst being educated in England and is buried beside St Nicholas parish church at Moreton. His homeland was in central America, in Belize and the islands of the Bay of Honduras, where the friendly connections between the natives and the British caused resentment in Washington and disputes with the United States during the 1860s.

During his 'wilderness years' before the Second World War, Winston Churchill led mourners from this church, following the bier carrying Lawrence of Arabia, to the village churchyard around the corner, in May 1935.

Colonel Thomas Edward Lawrence (1888–1935), who lived at nearby Clouds Hill from 1923, rallied the Desert Revolt of Bedouin Arabs against the Turks during the Palestine campaign of 1917–18.

The creation of Lawrence's colourful media image – dressed as a Prince of Mecca in an heroic and romantic contrast to carnage and reality on the Western Front – was largely due to American movie-maker Lowell Thomas. President Woodrow Wilson sent Thomas across Europe and the Middle East on a ground-breaking mission to prepare a news-reel record of the First World War.

The Georgian apse of Moreton parish church which has been the scene of funerals for princes of the Mosquitoes and Mecca.

NETHER COMPTON

The Tiddy Caves

Gore Lane, Stallen – ST 603 168

Man-made caverns carved out of the sandy cliffs beside deep-cut lanes between Stallen and Nether Compton, in the hills between Sherborne and Yeovil, date back to Elizabethan and Jacobean times. They were dug as potato stores.

The tubers of white potatoes, grown by Incas in the Chilean Andes, were tasted by Sir Francis Drake in 1577 during his circumnavigation of the globe. In 1586, Drake failed to intercept a Spanish treasure fleet in the Caribbean but took possession of potatoes that were being carried as ship's stores. These found their way, via traders commissioned by Sir Walter Raleigh, to Virginia, Ireland and England. Harriot, his agent, is said to have handed Raleigh potato seed rather than tubers in 1590 – from Youghal in south-west Ireland – so the mariner's first taste of the offering was an adverse gourmet experience.

Because of the Raleigh connection, when he was living at Sherborne Castle, the crop was first grown in England on the light soils to the west of Sherborne. After being dug, the potatoes have to be stored in cool, dark conditions – to prevent them turning green and poisonous – which seems to have presented something of a problem to the first English growers. They solved it by digging a series of caves into sandstone banks where ancient lanes slice through the landscape.

The restored Tiddy Cave in Gore Lane, Stallen, near Nether Compton.

The best surviving cave, beside Gore Lane and beneath the land of farmer Roger Foot, was restored in 1997 by masons Les Evans and John Starkes of Lillington Construction in a project backed by West Dorset District Council.

Two more views of the restored Tiddy Cave in Gore Lane, Stallen, near Nether Compton.

PIDDLEHINTON

Piddlehinton Camp

Bourne Park and Enterprise Park – SY 723 967

Piddlehinton Camp, as it approached the last Christmas of the Second World War, was suddenly evacuated. Eighty acres of huts, housing a total of 5000 American infantrymen, was left a winter waste-land as, to their dismay, the young men found that instead of celebrating the festivities they were sailing to war. Many of their young admirers, some soon to realise that they were pregnant, were left with a month of memories as the 66th Infantry Division of the United States Army headed for Southampton.

Half the camp survives in the same time-warp limbo, with Corfe Mullen entrepreneur Alan Perry being its latter day saviour as he restores the NAAFI where Glenn Miller played and converts lines of brick-built huts into business units that preserve the history, which progressed through a Gypsy camp stage to a refuge for Vietnamese boat-people.

Much better this, bringing new life to the Piddle Valley, than that the camp should be razed to the ground and returned at great expense to serve as second-rate agricul-tural land. As for the Americans, they had arrived on 26 November 1944 and were designated as back-up troops for the clear-up of Germans from the Bretagne penin-sula, in order to capture the U-boat pens at Brest.

Ironically, it was one of those vessels, *U-486*, that would cause a disaster. Fate was also cruel, and kind even to those prematurely disembarked, when the troops occupying the 11,500-ton Belgian liner *Leopoldville* at Southampton were changed over on the afternoon of 23 December. Her new complement, 2237 of them, were the 262nd Regiment and the 264th Regiment of the 66th Infantry Division.

The troopship sailed from Southampton Docks at 09.00 hours on Christmas Eve. Cards and the odd

mouth-whistle, wetted by a pint of beer apiece, were the only seasonal spirit. Likewise aboard the *Cheshire*, with more troops, and their escort destroyers HMS *Brilliant* and HMCS *Anthony*. It was off Spithead, at 11.00 hours, that they rendezvoused with another Canadian destroyer, HMCS *Holtern*, and the Free French frigate *Croix de Lorraine*. They went onto a war footing on passing at 14.00 a point in the English Channel that was codenamed 'PC' and commonly known as Piccadilly Circus. With the sight of the white cliffs of St Catherine's Point and the Isle of Wight behind them and almost out of sight, the convoy was ordered to increase speed and weave in a zig-zag pattern to avoid encounters with a German Submarine.

One was then detected, or suspected, as a 'ping' on *Brilliant*'s asdic screen. She raised a warning flag as the convoy ploughed on into heavier seas. The combat watch, in an intensely cold wind, was relaxed at 14.30 hours.

'Bunk duty' was the order of the *Leopoldville* as the men tried to recover from disrupted sleep amid bouts of seasickness. The crump of depth charges disturbed them at 15.20 as the destroyers reacted to their second U-boat alert. Nothing appeared to have been hit.

By 17.45, the convoy charted a course that brought it 5.5 miles north-east of the Allied-occupied port of Cherbourg, where its lights proclaimed confidence that wartime blackouts were now beyond their time. The place seemed to be having a party; which it was, this first Christmas of Liberation.

Then came the fatal torpedo, into the stern of the *Leopoldville*, on the starboard side – which was facing the open sea. She would take a couple of hours to sink, though when she did the liner went down fast, within ten minutes of the pressure of water bursting the bulkheads. Meanwhile, lifeboats were lowered and HMS *Brilliant* had led a rescue operation that should have won medals, but help expected from partying Cherbourg never arrived.

Wincanton solicitor J. Fenton Rutter, who was at sea off Cherbourg in an American LST (Landing Ship Tanks) on Christmas Eve, told me that many of the casualties resulted from complacency aboard the *Leopoldville*, ranging from failure to prepare for the event of having to evacuate the ship, down to the potentially fatal detail that many soldiers had no idea of how to fasten their life-jackets with the result that they became nooses around their necks. He quoted author John Harding: 'The troops should have been told to cross arms over the chest so that on hitting the life preserver would not lift up and snap the neck.'

The LST was tasked to take Fenton Rutter from Cherbourg to Portsmouth but the crew had other ideas:

'The captain decided to delay departure for five hours and when he left he sailed to Weymouth in order to keep a date with a girl friend there. So I finished up in Weymouth. Some time beforehand I had taken passage on the fateful Leopoldville *and I remember at that time that the only instructions were to assemble on deck in case of an emergency.'*

When they woke up to reality on Christmas Day the Americans passed the buck back to the *Brilliant* and blamed the escort warships for the debacle. A total of 802 Americans were drowned, killed or missing presumed dead. Survival time in the icy waters was minutes rather than hours. When families in the United States received telegrams reporting their losses these were worded 'missing in action' and had to be followed by a second series of cables which confirmed the deaths.

Lawrence Bond, an American foreign correspondent in Paris, has researched the sinking for a documentary film. The wreck of the *Leopoldville* has been surveyed by divers Mike and Penny Rowley. It lies on its port side and the highest point is in 38 metres of water. The hull, superstructure and bridge are remarkably intact.

Poignantly, its bows point towards Cherbourg, and the visible damage is the impact hole caused by the torpedo and the crumpled stern behind it. The loss would be overshadowed by another disaster over that final wartime Christmas. To the east, at the other extremity of the front-line, the Germans had broken through the snowy forests of the Ardennes in their last great counter-offensive of the war. Their story became a legend of book and screen, remembered as the Battle of the Bulge, whereas the loss of the *Leopoldville* is hardly known.

An attempt to have a memorial provided for them, at Piddlehinton for the fiftieth anniversary, came to nothing. To add insult to injury, it was then found, instead, that the most poignant surviving relic of their short stay had been torn down. It was the bus shelter that they had waited at for trips to what night-life Dorchester could offer. Then, however, Alan Perry of Perry and Perry and Mark Berridge of Crendon Timber, decided to make sure that the sixtieth anniversary was commemorated in style.

They planted 802 beech trees on the slope above Enterprise Park, at former Piddlehinton Camp, and held a service of dedication in memory of those who died. The United States was represented by Lieutenant-Colonel Rich Gibbons, deputy defence attaché from the American Embassy in Grosvenor Square, and for its flag was a wartime standard from Weymouth which was given honourable centre-place in the colour party provided by the Royal British Legion.

Wartime guardroom (left) *and gate at Piddlehinton Camp.*

West Country Television filming surviving Nissen huts amid an expanse of wartime tarmac in December 2004, on the 60th anniversary of the loss of the Leopoldville.

Parade ground and the camp cinema where Glenn Miller played in the spring of 1944.

Alan Perry (left) *and Lieutenant-Colonel Rich Gibbons at Piddlehinton Camp, commemorating the sixtieth anniversary of the sinking of the* Leopoldville, *Christmas 2004.*

POOLE

Newfoundland traders

Old Town – SZ 008 904

The finest Georgian houses, around St James's parish church in the heart of Poole's Old Town, were the homes of the merchants who ran the fisheries on the Grand Banks off Newfoundland. Dozens of vessels were based in Poole. This long distance run, 2500 miles west-south-west to the featureless fogs on the far side of the Atlantic Ocean, had grown in scale towards the end of the sixteenth century. Cargoes included cod, cod-oil, copper ore, furs, preserved lobsters, salmon, seal-oil, sealskins and whale products.

The island of Newfoundland, one third larger than Ireland, formally became England's first overseas colony, in 1583. Cape Race lies only 1650 miles from Cape Clear which therefore form the closest transatlantic points between America and Europe. An island-hopping connection, via Iceland, was first made by Norsemen, who were landing on Newfoundland before the year 1000.

John Cabot, with a crew of 18 in the *Matthew* from Bristol, landed somewhere on the shore of North America – apparently the north-east coast of Newfoundland – and raised the banner of St George for King Henry VII, on 24 June 1497. Gaspar Corte Real, a sailor from the Azores, rediscovered Newfoundland in 1500. Portuguese and French fishermen began landing there each summer to cure their catches ashore. At the end of the American War of Independence, in the Paris peace talks of November 1782, Yankee negotiator John Adams forced the British to concede that American fishermen could continue to 'enjoy their ancient liberty to land and dry fish' on the coast of Newfoundland.

The Grand Banks form the greatest submarine plateau on the globe. Its notorious fogs arise from condensation of warm, moist air accompanying the Gulf Stream,

on meeting arctic currents from Baffin's Bay. Covering an area larger than Italy, the Grand Banks were the largest cod and seal fisheries on the planet, with an open season from June to November. Fish were caught in their hundreds on baited lines.

By the eighteenth century their importance was being reflected and represented by Poole's architecture, beginning with a 1704-dated merchant's house at No. 87 High Street, and No. 13 Thames Street which dates from about 1730. Hamburg merchant Sir Peter Thomson's house, in Market Street, was built between 1746 and 1749. This was the high-water point of the Newfoundland trade which continued to flourish for the next six decades. The American connection was boosted and sustained by the Napoleonic Wars, which disrupted contact with the continent, and the corollary was that peace brought poverty.

From 1815, with European free trade becoming a reality, the cold winds of competition reduced Poole to a regional port, visited by coasters and catering for low-value bulk freight such as clay and timber. It remained of a lesser importance, in national terms, until the advent of roll-on, roll-off ferries and a new wave of tariff-free trade when Britain joined the European Economic Community in the late twentieth century.

The Waterfront Museum, on the Quay, commemorates the town's time as Britain's main Atlantic fishing port. Outgoing vessels, to Newfoundland, took coal, cottons, cutlery, flour, nets, molasses and woollens. Newfoundland's imports, to the value of £1,400,000 in 1900, were funded in the main by exports of fish, to a total of £1 million, chiefly cod.

Because of the cherished connections between Newfoundland and England, and St John's and Poole in particular, the island of Newfoundland and the adjacent mainland coast of Labrador were the only parts of British North America which refused to join the Dominion of Canada on 1 July 1867, and stayed under Whitehall control until after the Second World War. One of the issues was the Royal Navy's former base at Argentia which had been transferred to the United States in part exchange for 50 'mothballed' destroyers which were released to Britain ahead of the Lend-Lease Act.

Newfoundland is to Canada what Pembrokeshire is to Wales, with both being regarded as a 'Little England', and it is easier to spot traditional Poole family names in St John's directories than in present-day equivalents back home.

William Taylor Haly

St James's Church — SZ 008 904

William Taylor Haly (1816–74) was born in Poole and is buried in its cemetery. In his boyhood he travelled with his father, Lieutenant Robert Standish Haly RN, in the Caribbean, and then stayed in the United States.

Robert Haly protested against the press-gang, which was impressing merchant seamen into naval service, with a 40-page publication on *Impressment; an Attempt to Prove Why it Should and How it Could be Abolished*. William Haly also established a reputation as 'an extreme radical' and went on to write 'a perfect encyclopaedia of political knowledge' which was how *The Times* praised his book on *The Opinions of Sir Robert Peel* in 1843.

Philip Henry Gosse

Skinner Street — SZ 013 904

Canadian zoologist Philip Henry Gosse (1810–88) began his career by collecting sea-anemones in Poole Harbour. The family had moved to Gosse House, Skinner Street, Poole, in 1812. As a young man, Philip worked his passage to Newfoundland and established himself in whaling offices there, using his spare time to put the colony's insect life under the microscope. He was the first to do so. Having moved on to Canada he compiled the *Entomology of Newfoundland*, an unpublished manuscript, in 1836. Further travels and studies did go into print, with the *Canadian Naturalist* of 1841 being followed by *An Introduction to Zoology* in 1843, *Birds of Jamaica* in 1847, and *A Naturalist's Sojourn* (in Jamaica) in 1851.

Back in the Old World, he described *The Antiquities of Assyria* in 1852, and *A Naturalist's Rambles on the Devonshire Coast* in 1853. This, and his earlier Poole discoveries, led to The Manual of Marine Biology in 1855–56 for which he produced 700 woodcut illustrations.

Then he jumped into the evolutionary debate with *Life* in 1857 and *Omphalos* in 1857 before tidying his boyhood sea-anemone notes into *Actinologia Britannicus*, between 1858 and 1860, which was the first standard work on the subject.

Letter from Alabama, in 1859, also recalled his well-travelled younger days. *In the Romance of Natural History*, published in 1860, he put forward the notion that the sea-serpent of world-wide mariners' tales was a Plesiosaur. *A Year at the Shore* in 1864 and *Land at Sea* in 1865 rounded off his main literary output and in retirement in Devon, increasingly though willingly constrained by his Plymouth Brethren beliefs, he grew orchids and drew almost microscopic plates of rotifers, the minute wheel animalcules. Philip was the father of Sir Edmund Gosse (1849–1928), his only child, who was born in London and found fame as a literary critic, author of *Father and Son*, and friend to Thomas Hardy.

United States Coast Guard plaque

East Quay – SZ 015 903

A plaque on East Quay, at the eastern end of Poole Quay, carries an etching of a high-speed launch to commemorate the life-saving support facilities for the American landings on Omaha Beach. The D-Day assault force was trailed by a fleet of United States Coast Guard cutters which carried out sterling service then and during the subsequent Battle of Normandy. The plaque was the idea of New Jersey carpet retailer Jack Campbell (born 1924) who raised $1000 from fellow veterans who had sailed from Poole and present members of the service. He handed over the plaque to Mayor Bruce Grant-Braham in February 1994:

'From this Quay, 60 cutters of the United States Coast Guard Rescue Flotilla 1 departed for the Normandy Invasion, 6 June 1944. These 83-foot boats, built entirely of wood, and the 840 crew members were credited with saving the lives of 1437 men and one woman. In remembrance of the service rendered by Rescue Flotilla 1, and with appreciation of the kindness of the people of Poole to the crews, this plaque is given by men and women of the United States Coast Guard.'

Coast Guard cutter featured on the quayside memorial to United States Coast Guard Rescue Flotilla 1 which sailed from Poole, to save the lives of 1437 men and one woman off Normandy, in 1944.

POOLE HARBOUR

Transatlantic flying-boats

Salterns Pier – SZ 035 895

The great expanse of landlocked water in south-east Dorset, the second largest natural harbour in the world, was from 1940 to 1945 Britain's principal international airport. Flying-boats of British Overseas Airways Corporation (formed by merging Imperial Airways with British Airlines in 1939) maintained the links to the Empire and North America. The first chairman of BOAC was Lord Reith, who as John Reith had been the iconic founding director-general of the BBC, and was Member of Parliament for Southampton until being created 1st Baron Reith of Stonehaven in 1940.

Before emergency re-location to the water runways of Poole Harbour – known as 'Trots' – they had been operating from Hythe and Calshot on Southampton Water. The Short S.23 Empire flying-boat *Cambria* had inaugurated the air-mail service to Canada and the United States in August 1939.

Despite the move westwards, to take the flying-boats away from major shipping lanes and disperse targets over a wider area, the Battle of Britain soon brought the war to Poole as well as Southampton. Even so, the first wartime transatlantic air-crossing took place secretly and successfully, when flying-boat *Clare* took off from Poole Harbour on 4 August 1940. *Clare's* second crossing from Poole, on 14 August 1940, carried Air Ministry Under-Secretary Captain Harold Balfour, who went to the States to buy three Boeing 314 Vale Clipper flying-boats. He found that six were being completed for Pan American Airways, intended for use in the Pacific, and did a deal with Juan Tripp of Pan-Am to acquire three of them.

Weighing 86,000 pounds, and being virtually double the size of the British C-class Empire flying-boats, they had a non-stop range of more than 4000 miles. The cost was $1,035,400 each, plus 12 spare 1600 horse-power Wright Cyclone engines at $16,753 each and six spare airscrews at $3625 each.

The unauthorised Washington bargain made by a mere Under-Secretary for $3,328,986 caused Treasury protests in London but Sir Archibald Sinclair defended his deputy from an angry Sir Kingsley Wood and the arrangement was confirmed. The long-range American aircraft roared into Poole towards the end of the year. They became the mainstay of VIP world travel and Prime Minister Winston Churchill returned in one, from the United States to Scotland, in 1942. Captain Balfour kept his job and retired eventually as Baron Balfour of Inchrye.

The Clippers were vital as wartime transports on the Empire 'Horseshoe Route' to South Africa, Arabia and India. From there the Royal Air Force ran a link to Ceylon and Australia. The problem with the smaller British flying-boats was that they needed to put down at Lisbon in neutral Portugal in order to re-fuel. This was acceptable for civilian passengers but not for service personnel though as it became obvious that the war was reaching its close diplomatic niceties attracted a Nelsonian blind eye.

All eastbound Clippers crossing the Atlantic during the conflict were required by the Irish Government to land at Foynes before proceeding to Poole. On arrival the flying-boat spent only two hours at Poole before taking off again, westbound, to re-cross the Atlantic. This was in order to keep the valuable and vulnerable aircraft on the waters of Poole Harbour for the shortest possible time. Having just flown 3247 nautical miles, the Clipper then returned across the same route, and in an average week the three British Clippers flew 12,988 miles between them.

The standard European route from Baltimore was via Botwood, Newfoundland, but Captain David Brice told *The Aeroplane* magazine that his pilots had considerable flexibility in the event of severe head-winds or fog-banks, 'because they could always "flight-plan" for Stephenville on the west coast of Newfoundland, or Shediac in New Brunswick, or even Dartmouth and Sydney, in Nova Scotia and Cape Breton islands, respectively. The crossing from Botwood to Foynes was 1,761 miles, cruising at 8000 feet.

The Clipper carried 3721 gallons of fuel and a payload of 3238 kilos. Heading east was the easy way around the globe as the jet stream generally assists the flight, Captain Brice explained:

'Due to prevailing westerly winds throughout the year, a zero wind component was allowed for, involving a flight time of 13.1 hours. To this an additional five hours' reserve [of fuel] was added. That this computation of the wind component was accurate is proved by the fact that only one aircraft throughout the season was delayed or returned because of adverse winds on this section.

'On many occasions aircraft arrived over Foynes with sufficient fuel to proceed to Poole direct, and would have done so, but for an agreement with the Eire Government which required all eaastbound aircraft to alight at Foynes. In several cases weather conditions did fall below the miniumum landing conditions, when the aircraft was beyond the point of no return, making a direct flight from Botwood to Poole a necessity.'

Heading westbound, however, was another matter. Much more fuel had to be used to battle the winds, which averaged 25 knots, and at 4000 feet the 'endurance' was 17.8 hours with reserve fuel for another five hours. Sometimes this was insufficient to reach Botwood, or Clippers arrived in blizzards or fog, or suffered mechanical troubles, in which case they put down at Shediac, Stephenville or Dartmouth, near Halifax.

Making up for the cursory checks on arrival at Poole, having returned to Baltimore each flying-boat was given a fifty-hour inspection on the water, and after each 200 hours flying time they were beached and taken into the hangar for a full mechanical service.

In 1945 there were two scheduled weekly services from Poole Harbour, both operated by the British Overseas Airways Corporation, with one still using the Clipper flying-boats. This was to Baltimore, though now via Africa, across the Equitorial narrows of the South Atlantic. Stopping points were Lisbon, Bathurst, Natal (Brazil), Belem, Trinidad and Bermuda.

The other route was operated by 22 British Short S.23 C-class Empire flying-boats, a civilian conversion of the basic military Sunderland III airframe. The fleet included its veteran prototype, *Canopus*, which became the first of the line on joining Imperial Airways, in October 1936. She had now flown for 15,000 hours and covered 2,000,000 miles.

The Empire service headed generally south-eastwards, to the Middle East and South-East Asia, calling at Biscarosse, Augusta, Cairo, Bahrein, Karachi, Calcutta and Rangoon following its liberation from the Japanese in May 1945. Long-distance travellers from Poole, to the Air Transport Conference in New Zealand on 21 February 1946, included Lord Winster (Minister for Civil Aviation) and Lord Knollys (Chairman of BOAC). They led the British delegation.

The Clippers were withdrawn from service in the spring of 1946. By the time the war had ended each had flown more than a million miles on the trans-Atlantic service. Their figures, issued in October 1945, were 1,100,513 miles for *Bristol*, 1,066,983 miles for *Bangor*, and 1,030,529 miles for *Berwick*. The basic frequency was once a week in each direction on a standard wartime route that headed for the equator when outward bound but returned along a direct path to complete the circuit. Westbound: Poole – Lisbon – Bathurst – Belem – Trinidad – Bermuda – Baltimore. Eastbound: Baltimore – Bermuda – Lisbon – Poole.

The last scheduled flights were from Baltimore on 4 March and Poole on 7 March 1946. They continued in use, on the Atlantic seaboard, between Baltimore and Bermuda on a twice-weekly service. This had started on 18 October 1945. No passport was required from United States citizens, who were offered their first chance for a post-war overseas holiday by air, at £41 for the return fare.

Salterns Pier at Lilliput, the main land-link for the Dorset operation, was handed back to Poole Yacht Club. Flying-boats were being replaced by Lockheed Constellations as the mainstay of international aviation.

Flying-boat Clare having returned to Poole Harbour from the first transatlantic flight of the Second World War, in August 1940, though this photograph has been censored (left background) to delete details that would have revealed the location.

Clipper-class flying-boats of Pan American Airways featured on pre-war British cigarette cards.

Boeing Clipper flying-boat G-AGBZ Bristol *of British Airways on a mooring in Poole Harbour as a launch comes alongside with travellers for New York in 1945.*

PORTLAND

John Penn

Pennsylvania Castle – ST 696 711

John Penn (1760–1834), grandson of William Penn – the founder of Pennsylvania – was governor of the Isle and Royal Manor of Portland. In 1803 he built a seaside mansion, designed as a mock-fortress, on its eastern cliffs above Church Ope Cave. Pennsylvania Castle, designed by eminent architect James Wyatt, stands among the sycamore trees of Portland's only wood.

The eldest surviving son of Thomas Penn, John inherited his father's properties in 1775, including the moiety of the proprietorship of Pennsylvania, with its hereditary governorship, and Stoke Poges Park, Buckinghamshire. John Penn went to Pennsylvania in 1782 and stayed there until 1789, building a home called Solitude at Schuylkill. Along with his cousin, another John Penn (1729–95), he was granted £15,000 a year by the Assembly on account of the estate being forfeited to the Commonwealth of Pennsylvania under legislation passed on 18 January 1786. On returning to England, in the 1790s, he received a Parliamentary annuity in compensation for his overall losses in America.

As governor of Portland from 1805, and commandant of the strategically-placed Royal Portland Legion during the Napoleonic Wars, the unmarried John Penn gave particular thought to advising others on their liaisons and relationships. Nothing seems to have resulted from a poem entitled 'Marriage' which was published anonymously in the *Monthly Magazine* in 1815. Penn then went public with his concerns, forming a Matrimonial Society over the winter of 1816. By May 1817 this had changed its name to the Outinian Society and was holding meetings in Penn's London house at No. 10 New Street, Spring Gardens.

These gatherings progressed to the stately surroundings of Stoke Park where Penn gave lectures and edited the society's proceedings in his private press at Stoke Poges. The society was still in existence in 1825 though by then he had moved on to the stage. His play on the victory of King Alfred over Guthrum, the Dane, entitled *The Battle of Eddington*, or *British Liberty*, went to several editions and was performed both at Windsor and Covent Garden in 1824, and enjoyed a revival at Sadler's Wells Theatre in 1832.

After his death at Stoke Park, on 21 June 1834, Pennsylvania Castle passed to John's brother, Granville Penn (1761–1844). Granville's lifelong interest in apocalyptic prophecy had led him, in 1822, to mount an academic backlash against the emerging science of the times, by turning the book of Genesis into a manual of geology with *A Comparative Estimate of the Mineral and Mosaical Geologies*.

Pennsylvania Castle briefly passed to Granville's sons, Granville John Penn (1802–67) and Thomas Gordon Penn (1803–69), followed by their cousin, William Stuart, who transferred it to another close relative, Colonel Stewart Forbes. It still contained its historic contents when it was bought by J. Merrick Head in 1887.

After a period as Pennsylvania Castle Hotel, the clifftop mansion became a private home once more, latterly for multi-millionaire lawyer Stephen Curtis (1958–2004), who ran the troubled Russian oil firm Menatep. He had taken over from ousted oligarch Platon Lebedev who was arrested in 2003 on charges of fraud and tax evasion. Having told an uncle he would be dead 'within two weeks' and that 'it would be no accident', Stephen Curtis was killed a fortnight later with his pilot, Max Radford (thirty-four), on 3 March 2004.

Their helicopter which was based at Bournemouth Airport, Hurn, crashed while they were en route from Curtis's Mayfair offices to his home on Portland. An accident investigation blamed a navigation error, caused by poor weather, but the pilot's father, Dennis Radford (seventy-two) insisted at the inquest before Bournemouth coroner Mr Sherrif Payne, in 2005, that the possibility of sabotage had not been properly invesitgated and that airport secruity at Hurn was lax.

Pennsylvania Castle, built by a descendant of the founding father, on Portland's eastern cliffs.

William Penn's jewellery cabinet, photographed at Pennsylvania Castle, in May 1921.

PORTLAND

Exercise Tiger

off Portland Bill – SY 677 683

Though the wartime Exercise Tiger of April 1944 took place at Slapton Sands, Devon, the catastrophic loss of two United States LSTs (Landing Ships Tank) to German E-boats occurred in the eastern sector of Lyme Bay, 6 miles west-south-west of Dorset's most seaward point at Portland Bill.

The wreck of *LST 531* lies at latitude 50 degrees 26 minutes 8 seconds north, longitude 2 degrees 43 minutes 39 seconds west (Decca reading purple E70.08, red F2.72). That of *LST 507* is at latitude 50 degrees 26 minutes 8 seconds north, longitude 2 degrees 44 minutes 1 second west (Decca reading purple E70.08, red F1.73).

My primary informant for the true account of the tragic events of the early hours of 28 April 1944 has been Leading Telephonist Nigel Cresswell, retired and living in Wimborne, who was the twenty-year-old senior wireless operator in Motor Torpedo Boat 701. He was serving with the 63rd MTB Flotilla and had just returned to Portland Harbour from patrols into enemy-occupied French waters that had extended over three consecutive nights. The story began on the morning of the previous day as Allied forces in Tor Bay and Lyme Bay prepared for rehearsals of the D-Day landings on Slapton Sands.

Nigel Cresswell received a visit from a Wren Radio Mechanic, who he named as June Caswell:

'Her surname is almost the same as mine. She had a long face and I asked what was wrong. June replied that her American boyfriend had told her he was going on an exercise with landing craft in Lyme Bay. I asked her where she had been told that and she replied that it was in a Weymouth pub.'

MTB 701, along with five others of the 63rd MTB Flotilla, were on stand-by at Portland Naval Base on 27 April.

'Later that afternoon I was called to the Skipper's cabin and informed that the Senior Officer of the 63rd had offered the flotilla to escort some LSTs who were to be on exercise in Lyme Bay. The dockyard buzz was that the sole escort was to be a veteran V&W class destroyer from the Royal Navy. This proved to be nearly correct as HMS Scimitar, a British destroyer of the Great War, was assigned to protect Convoy T-4. But on the morning of 27 April she put into Plymouth Naval Base for repairs to slight damage to her bows, arising from a collision with a LCI [Landing Craft Infantry] the previous night, in Tor Bay.'

In the evening, Mr Cresswell heard that his Senior Officer's offer of the 63rd's services had been rejected by an American officer, which as he realised in retrospect was to prove a costly and disastrous decision.

The only protection for the LSTs was a single Flower-class corvette, HMS *Azalea* of 925 tons and just two guns (one 4-inch and a pom-pom). The closest other Allied warships were more than 15 miles away. The convoy therefore offered an irresistible target for torpedo attack by opportunistic German E-boats that duly ran amok.

The losses were 441 dead from the United States Army; 197 dead from the United States Navy; 'a handful' of dead Royal Artillery Bofors gunners; plus an unknown quantity of injured men.

LST 531 and *LST 507* were sunk by torpedoes. *LST 289* was hit by a torpedo and limped westwards to safety in Dartmouth. *LST 511* was damaged by gunfire and escaped the other way, around Portland Bill, into Weymouth Bay. The rest of Convoy T-4 scattered and survived.

The one-sided battle had been watched by Royal Artillerymen of the Coast Defence Battery at Blacknor

Fort, high on Portland's western cliffs to the south of Tout Quarry, who reported that the German E-boats were within range but coastal defences were ordered not to open fire, due to the number of Allied personnel fighting for their lives in the water. It was about 03.00 hours on 28 April that alarm bells rang in Portland Naval Base and the crews of the two 63rd Flotilla MTBs resting in Portland Harbour were woken and ordered to put to sea as Nigel recalls:

'MTB 701's engines were warmed up and myself and Telegraphist Ken Leigh switched on both our Wireless Telegraphy [W/T] sets. There was a fair amount of W/T traffic on the longer distance receiving set but it was all in code; a code that Coastal Forces boats were not issued with. The high frequency W/T set, an American TCS set, provided no traffic at all even though we tried all the crystals provided for pre-set tuning.'

After an hour or so, *MTB 701* was stood down, but only for a couple of hours. The ship's log reveals that they 'slipped from jetty at 06.45, passed the harbour gate at 07.00, proceeded at 21 knots on various courses into Lyme Bay'. The log ceases at 07.39.

In retirement, Nigel Cresswell received a letter from his wartime Navigator, confirming that *MTB 701* had nosed her way through floating bodies and brought four or five on board for identification. Nigel's own memories, as ever, are vivid:

'On a bright, sunny late spring morning I saw us approach what looked like an outdoor swimming pool, but there were hundreds of bodies in the water and they were all dead. I was not quite 21 and had seen the odd dead body, but nothing to what we saw before us. It had a profound effect on us young men and I will never forget it, ever. I remember examining two or three bodies that had been brought on board. Their Army denim uniforms had the buttons crimped to the material so that the buttons could not be removed. I remember two of the dog tags had 'Rome City, New York.'

'Their life-jackets were different from ours, with two circular rings sewn together with a small cylinder of gas at one end. When depressed the life-jacket would inflate. We were ordered by another MTB to return the bodies to the water and in a letter to me, Able Seaman Torpedoman Wood said that

we were supposed to puncture the life jackets as we had seen too much. I do distinctly remember seeing a very few bodies in the water wearing British Army khaki battledress with the square red badges of Royal Artillerymen.'

On the evening of 28 April, *MTB 701* joined the five other boats of the 63rd in their usual patrol 'on the other side' – cross-Channel to the Channel Islands and Cherbourg peninsula – and returned to Portland on the morning of 29 April. Nigel Cresswell walked through the dockyard to try and see his current girlfriend, Wren Torpedo Mechanic Doreen Smedley. He was told that these Wrens were not about:

'Looking into the Torpedo Workshop from a distance of a few yards I saw lots of shrouded bodies. I was quickly ushered away.'

Immediately after the disaster, the Allied High Command instituted a total blackout of the event. Survivors were dispersed to various service hospitals along the South Coast, but not before the medical staff had been briefed to avoid inquiring into the circumstances of their injuries. The penalty for breaking this injunction would be courts martial.

There were serious consequences for the D-Day secret, which could have been compromised, as 20 United States officers with the classification of 'BIGOT' had to be accounted for. These men knew not only when but where the invasion of Europe would take place and its sector names of Utah and Omaha. General Dwight D. Eisenhower, the Supreme Commander Allied Expeditionary Force, had given strict instructions that no Bigot-classified personnel should go on any operation before D-Day, in case they were captured by the Germans. This may explain the subsequent cover-up.

Having the E-boats credited with an heroic attack on massed Allied invasion craft and 30 Allied warships up to the size of cruiser, off Slapton Sands in mid-Devon did not break the Eisenhower edict. Had the true location been admitted, 50 miles to the east and within sight of Portland Bill, then not only had Eisenhower been defied but questions would have been asked as to why such a risky exercise had been mounted. Not merely was the sole escort a corvette, but the manoeuvring of the LSTs could have revealed the route and battle-plan of D minus one and D-Day itself.

A disaster was nearly a calamity. To this day there is uncertainty about the disposal of the 650 bodies, with a memorial having been erected over what are said to be graves at Slapton Sands, as others claim that they were buried in underground galleries and storage shafts below Verne Prison on Portland which were sealed before the closure of the Royal Navy base in the 1990s.

Lance-Corporal Tecwyn Morgan from Barry, South Wales, who was born in 1912, told me in 1999 that as a gunner in a coastal battery, stationed in a tent between Portland and Ferrybridge, he saw the corpses from LSTs being unloaded at Portland:

'We were sworn to secrecy. I saw bodies taken from LSTs which were moved into Balaclava Bay, outside Portland Harbour, as Delta Force was inside and they didn't want anyone to see the carnage. It has played on my mind for decades. Captain Murphy, who oversaw the clearing-up, had the bodies taken from Castletown and packed into tunnels. That is the reason, I'm sure, that the tunnels were collapsed by explosions before the Royal Navy departed in 1994.'

Invasion Force O

Portland Dockyard – SY 690 745

Castletown hards and the former Royal Navy Dockyard at Portland Harbour were the embarkation points for the tank landing craft and other American armour and engineer support that went with Force O (for Omaha) in the D-Day invasion of Normandy in June 1944.

As a war correspondent, the author Ernest Hemingway flew across the Atlantic on a VIP Pan American Airways' flight with actress Gertrude Lawrence in April 1944. After taken up residence in the Dorchester Hotel he travelled down to Weymouth at the end of May and joined the assault transport vessel USS *Dorothea L. Dix* in Portland Harbour on the evening of D-Day minus one which was that of Sunday 4 June. The invasion of Europe was delayed by bad weather, however, and they did not sail for another 24 hours, sailing for France overnight on 5-6 June 1944.

There, off Omaha Beach, he was transferred to an LCVP [Landing Craft Vital Personnel] commanded by Lieutenant Robert Anderson of Roanoke, Virginia, who delivered his charges to the Fox Green sector of the sands. Hemingway remained aboard and was then ferried back, under fire, to the relative safety of *Dorothea L. Dix*. He was hauled aboard by bosun's chair and returned with the vessel to England, and the Dorchester Hotel, Park Lane, where in the remains of the day he started writing his famous report from London for *Collier's Magazine* on 'how we took Fox Green Beach'.

The Hemingway myth machine then went into overdrive. By Hemingway's own account, Colleville and its church tower had only been pinpointed in the fog of war thanks to his photographic memory of maps and landmarks. He had then gone ashore with the men. More layers of fiction were added in the months that followed.

By the time the story had been relayed via William van Dusen, of the United States Navy, and then through the author's brother and biogrpaher, Leicester Hemingway, it had become the epic account of 'Hemingway's Longest Day'. He was credited with having led a company of combat troops towards a German pillbox and then having crawled back to the shore to tell the beach commander to bring reinforcements.

Portland's memorial to its American friends was unveiled after the war, in Victoria Gardens, by United States Ambassador John Gilbert Winant. He drove along Victory Road which had been named for the occasion. It was raining, which matched Gil Winant's mood, as he was tortured by unrequited love for Sarah Churchill, the wartime Prime Minister's daughter, and shot himself in 1947 after returning to New York

to be the United States representative to the new Union Nations.

Dorset's quarrying island has given its name to some 20 Portlands across the new world.

Fields of American armour, near Dorchester in May 1944, awaiting transit via Portland for the Battle of Normandy.

The United States 2nd Armored Division, casting aside training rounds in Dorset on 1 June 1944, in preparation for the imminent Channel crossing.

Left: *Landlady Elizabeth Comben* (centre) *of the Cove House Hotel, Portland, saying farewell to the United States Navy on 3 June 1944.*

Below: *American Engineer company approaching landing ships 374* (left) *and 376 on purpose-built hards at Castletown, Portland, on 4 June 1944.*

Castletown hards with United States landing ship 314 being loaded from the quay (top left) *and assault landing craft in the foreground.*

Portland embarkation with a fully-laden DUKW entering the jaws of American landing ship 376 at Castletown, Portland.

The ninth (near right) of a total of 12 vehicles being packed aboard United States landing craft 195 at Castletown, Portland, on 4 June 1944.

Left: *Reversed on – so that it could drive off forwards on beaching – half-track Brass City being loaded on to an American landing craft at Portland.*

Below: *The pointing finger of a single American GI (centre right) who has spotted the camera, breaking the monotony of the long wait beside Portland Harbour on D-Day minus One.*

Above: *Midway across, between Dorset and Normandy, showing a fraction of the Allied armada, with each vessel protected from air attack by a barrage balloon, at dawn on 6 June 1944.*

Left: *War correspondent Ernest Hemingway sailed from Portland Harbour aboard the troopship USS* Dorothea L. Dix *on D-Day.*

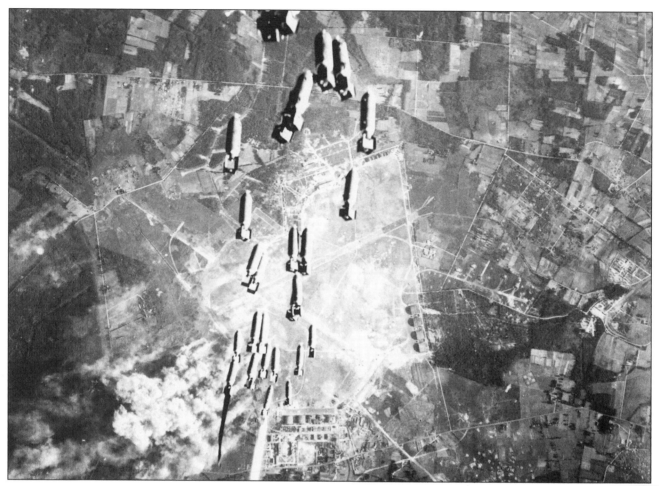

Bombs falling from 24,000 feet on to a Luftwaffe airfield near Bordeaux, on 15 June 1944, from one of the Flying Fortress bombers which crossed Dorset.

United States B-17 Flying Fortress bombers returning over Portland Harbour from a cross-channel mission after D-Day.

Depressing day in the rain for United States Ambassador Gil Winant, at the unveiling of Portland's D-Day memorial, on 22 August 1945.

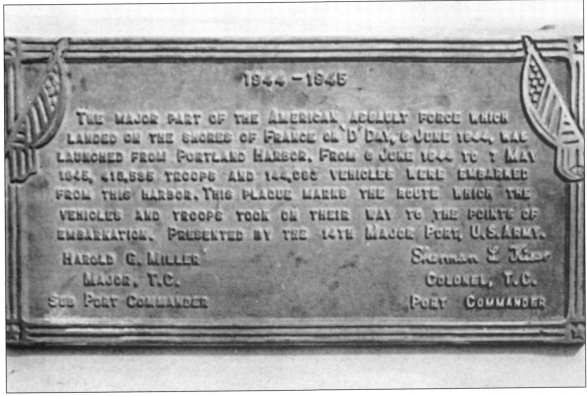

Portland plaque recording the pivotal part played by Portland in the invasion of Europe as 14th Major Port of the United States Army.

PORTLAND

USS *Nautilus*

Portland Naval Base – SY 695 747

The world's first nuclear submarine, which was built in 1954, surfaced in Weymouth Bay and arrived in Portland Harbour in October 1957 where she was welcomed to Britain by the First Sea Lord, Lord Louis Mountbatten, and Defence Minister Duncan Sandys who was preparing to take the Royal Navy down the nuclear path.

The crew of *Nautilus* were also making preparations, to return to Dorset, in triumph after an epic record-achieving voyage, across the entire northern hemisphere. Having set off from Pearl Harbor, Hawaii, the boat passed under the North Pole on 10 August 1958 and duly completed the arctic transit in Portland Harbour. She was later used as a research craft and is now preserved in a maritime museum at Groton, Connecticut.

Submarine 571, USS Nautilus, *entered New York for her first public appearance during Armed Forces Week in May 1956.*

RINGSTEAD

USAF Tropospheric Scatter Station

Ringstead Bay – SY 745 815

During the middle period of the Cold War, from the late 1950s through to the mid-1970s when it was rendered obsolete by satellite technology, the United States Air Force command signals between Britain and Spain were bounced via an ultra-shortwave Tropospheric Scatter Station beside Ringstead Bay. Great steel dishes overlooked the seaside path at Perry Ledge, between Ringstead and Osmington Mills, with huts and bunkers being tucked away in the under-growth of the wooded glens towards mediaeval Glebe Cottage and Spring Bottom..

A total of 200 acres had been requisitioned though the military use later shrank to 5 acres. In 1970, retired Canford schoolmaster Yvone Kirkpatrick, a veteran Royal Flying Corps pilot from the First World War who had a villa at Ringstead, explained what was still a top secret matter:

'Many repeat the fallacy of the Ringstead radar station, which it isn't! It is an ultra-shortwave station for the United States Air Force. Signals come from the command headquarters at High Wycombe via beacon masts within visual range. The last one at Bulbarrow transmits to Portland which re-transmits the signal to a mini-receiver at Ringstead. This arrangement is necessary because of the hills. The incoming signal is fed into the Ringstead transmitter which beams it to the Spanish border via the troposphere.'

Ultra-shortwave radio Tropospheric Scatter Station of the United States Air Force, beside Ringstead Bay, in 1968.

SHAFTESBURY

Richard Upjohn

Bimport – ST 861 230

Brookline Manor, in the fashionable Boston suburb, was designed by Shaftesbury-born Richard Upjohn (1802–78), the renowned first President of the American Institute of Architects.

Richard Upjohn was born at Shaftesbury on 22 January 1802, at an unknown address though it was said to have been near Holy Trinity Church, Bimport, which was rebuilt on its mediaeval site in 1842. Richard was the son of James Upjohn and Elizabeth Plantaganet Dryden Michell. The father was a surveyor, as were Richard's brothers, William and James. There had been Upjohns in Shaftesbury for generations. Thomas Upjohn appeared in the church register for 1680 when he married Ann Oran. They had distant Welsh origins (Upjohn being an anglicisation of Apjohn – 'son of John').

One John Upjohn, born in 1760, could have been the Dorset clockmaker of about 1700 who was rediscovered by Tom Tribe and Philip Whatmoor for their *Dorset Clocks and Clockmakers*. It seems quite possible as his sister, Anna, married a watchmaker, John Gilonne.

The mother of Richard Upjohn died of consumption only months after he was born. The family's first transatlantic encounter was in 1808 when James Upjohn senior sailed to Newfoundland, which had close Dorset connections through Poole and the fisheries, and spent a season or longer in a trading base there. Richard tried hard to establish himself in Shaftesbury, being apprenticed to Richard Downs, a cabinet-maker in the town, in 1819.

In November 1826 Richard Upjohn married Elizabeth Parry from Denbigh, North Wales, and the result was Richard Michell Upjohn, born on 7 March 1828.

Furniture making continued to be Richard's trade but he may have pursued extravagant taste and style, for soon the business was in deep trouble.

'The want of proper trust in Divine Providence, too much confidence in my own power, and too little knowledge of Mankind sent me foundering in difficulties in my native land,' he wrote about the period. An uncle's offer to pay the debts was refused, though the immediate problems were overcome:

'These I enabled to adjust and not being desirous of realising a second time that what I considered hard treatment from some of whom I ought to have received something better, I resolved without much reflection to sail for this country with my dear wife and child.'

The arrangements were made through Elizabeth's brother Richard Parry, who lived at Manlius in upstate New York. They sailed aboard the *Hebe*, from London. Richard Upjohn wote in his diary on 22 April 1829:

'Very pleasant now off the coast of Dorset, Portland bears about ten miles off, St Alban's [Head] is plain to be seen. In consequence of the wind last night, the sea rolls, makes the ship move from head to stern.'

The following day the wind was still favourable and Dorset slipped from sight:

'Ship goes about nine miles an hour. Wife very sick but not so much as some.'

They cast anchor in the quarantine ground off Staten Island on 31 May 1829 and were cleared for landing by an American doctor the following day.

Richard Upjohn later told his son:

'We walked up Broadway, your mother with pattens on her feet and a baby in her arms, and the first roof we went under was Trinity Church and ten years later I put a new roof on it.'

He arrived at Manlius with just three silver dollars in his pocket. Initially he was employed by a whale oil merchant, Samuel Leonard, as a draftsman and contractor at the close of 1830, when Leonard had successfully diversified into the construction business after a fire destroyed much of New Bedford. The title for which Richard is remembered was first added after his name on a Courthouse design of 1833 and he commented:

'If that's Architecture, then I am an Architect, and after that I hung out my shingle.'

This, effectively, was his first advertisement which appeared in the *New Bedford Daily Mercury* on 5 March 1833:

'Architectural Plans And Elevations, Neatly Executed At Short Notice, By Richard Upjohn. Orders Left At The Mechanics' Hall, New Bedford.'

Upjohn moved in 1834 to Boston and was employed by Alexander Parris, Architect of the city's St Paul's Cathedral. Soon he set up his own practice and quickly gained reputation as a designer of fine churches and handsome houses.

In January 1836 he became an American citizen and in 1837 he started work on rebuilding St John's at Bangor. The soaring gothic spire of another of Upjohn's churches – a spire which topped every building in New York for nearly fifty years – still provides press photographers with a favourite shot, for it closes the vista at the end of a chasm-like Wall Street. Only recently a London daily gave the shot the caption:

'God and Mammon'. In Upjohn's time it was observed that he built his churches in a 'purer and more artistic form of English Gothic than had previously been seen in America'.

With Trinity Church, from 1841 to 1846, he created the most acclaimed ecclesiastical building in North America. One New Yorker exclaimed:

'The glory of our city! The noblest in conception and the purest in detail of ecclesiastical structure in the country.'

Commisions piled up in Upjohn's office in Broadway and in 1850, at the pinnacle of his career, he left for a tour of Europe. The trip started with a return to Shaftesbury that restored his pride and credibility, taking back the final repayment of his debts in a silk purse made by his daughter. From then on he had enough work but was disappointed that many small companies could not afford even the most moderate of prices. This prompted him to publish, at his own expense, a handbook entitled *Upjohn's Rural Architecture* with designs that were essentially simple and inexpensive to build. He became one of the chief founders of the American Institute of Architecture, and with the unanimous acclamation of his fellows was elected its first President in 1857. He held this position until his retirement in 1876.

During this time he designed in the style of the Italian Renaissance and built mansions for rich clients in Cincinnati, Philadelphia, Buffalo, Tarrytown, Long Island and Newport. His own house was on Clifton Street, Brooklyn, and built by him while he was working on Trinity Church. In retirement he moved to Garrison-on-the-Hudson, living close to his little church of St Philip-in-the-Highlands, where he was buried in 1878.

Left: *Brookline Manor near Boston, Massachusetts, built in 1840 by Richard Upjohn from Shaftesbury, who became the first president of the American Institute of Architects.*

Below: *Richard Upjohn, the acclaimed New York architect, painted in about 1850 when he returned to Dorset to pay off the last of his debts.*

SHERBORNE

Sir Walter Raleigh

Old Castle and Sherborne Castle – ST 648 167 & 649 165

Both of Sherborne's historic castles were home to Sir Walter Raleigh (1552–1618). He was damp and uncomfortable in the Old Castle and therefore built the replacement Sherborne Castle to the south, on the site of a lodge, with landscaped grounds and a lake between them. The trees include some of the first cedars to be brought to England from Virginia.

Also in the grounds is the stone seat where Raleigh is said to have been smoking when an agitated servant, thinking he was on fire, threw a flagon of ale over his head – the sort of thing that happens today if you attempt smoking in New York.

Queen Elizabeth's favourite mariner, in her reign Raleigh never actually crossed the Atlantic but sent expeditions which explored the coast from Florida to North Carolina. He named it 'Virginia' in honour of the Virgin Queen in 1584, and organised various attempts at its settlement. As well as tobacco and trees, he was instrumental in bringing potatoes to Ireland and England.

Accused of conspiracy by Elizabeth's successor, James I, he was put in the Tower of London. The condition of his release was to search for gold along the Orinoco, but the voyage collapsed through storms, desertion and disease, including the death of his own son, Walter. Against orders he razed a Spanish town, and returned to have an earlier sentence of death carried out, being beheaded in Whitehall.

Above: *Sir Walter and Lady Raleigh in the Sherborne Pageant of 1905.*

Left: *Contemporary portrait of Sir Walter Raleigh.*

Left and below: *Raleigh's first home at Sherborne was the Old Castle.*

Right and below: *The present Sherborne Castle, across the lake from the Old Castle, was built by Raleigh as his second home.*

Above: *Raleigh's Seat, in Sherborne Park, is linked to the legend of the nation's first smoker.*

Left: *Virginia Ash, Henstridge, with a sign appropriate for a modern non-smoking establishment, showing a servant about to douse Raleigh's pipe.*

SHERBORNE

US 294th Engineer Company

Sherborne Park – ST 651 159

Revelations that came to light as a result of the American Freedom of Information Act show that an 'enemy agents' story was invented as a cover-up to conceal the fact that a combat exercise course had been laid out in Sherborne Park within the confines of the 228th Field Hospital Unit of the United States Army.

That meant the site of a massive explosion, at midday on Monday 20 March 1944, came under the auspices and protection of the International Red Cross under the terms of the Geneva Convention and should not have been used by armed personnel, nor for the storing of ammunition, let alone for the laying of a live mine-field. The colossal bang took place 500 yards south-south-east of Sherborne Castle, 50 yards on the Haydon side of Castleton public footpath number 6 which runs from home farm to the camp on the south side of Sherborne Park.

'It was a tremendous explosion, the loudest anyone had ever heard,' said sixteen-year-old Tod Frost who had been threshing a corn-rick beside a private road in front of Sherborne Castle and had a Land Army girl hurled on top of him in the straw, almost being impaled on her pitchfork. 'Bits of lorry and bodies were strewn across half a mile,' he said. One truck had totally disintegrated and others were mangled. Troops and ambulances from the nearby camp came to clear up:

'Open lorries passed along the road directly beneath us. We could see the rows of mutilated bodies covered with ground-sheets. It was an appalling sight.'

The number of casualties was variously given as 29 (now listed on the comemmorative plaque in Half Moon Street); 35 to 40; and up to 140. Betty Warner,

then aged twenty-three and living in Coombe, on the other side of the town, writes that 'the whole of Sherborne heard the explosion'. She recorded in her diary a death toll of 37, including her new-found friends Joseph B. Henning and Lucien P. Pessoz: 'Another American, Frank, came to tell us Joe and Lucien had been killed along with 35 others.'

All accounts agree that there were only bodies to be counted and no injuries to be tended.

The accident happened when a lorry slipped back onto a mine during clearing up after an exercise with anti-tank and anti-personnel mines by the United States 294th Engineer Company. The wheels came to rest on an 8-pound anti-tank mine, the bellows of which would have needed a pressure of 250-pounds to trigger detonation. That set off all the mines stacked in the truck.

What happened next was that a myth was spun. On realising the embarrassing illegality of the incident, because of the abuse of Hospital Camp status, a cover-story was invented. Sherborne Park, it was said, had been infiltrated by German agents who brought a truck-load of mines into an Army physical training course, with the culprits being named as Kurt Henlein and Ernst Buchner who would be executed at Salisbury, by the military, in May 1944.

Censorship and news management was the norm. Such manipulation was vital to avoid giving indications to the enemy of the size and disposition of the American Army – by this time 80,000 strong in the Dorset area – that had built up on the coast opposite the Cherbourg peninsula and Normandy beaches. Secrecy became a necessary cloak for incompetence.

STALBRIDGE

Revd George Rodgers

Congregational Chapel – ST 736 178

The self-styled 'President' of 'Yeovil Colony', which has since reverted to its native name of Muskoda, was Congregational minister Revd George Rodgers from Stalbridge. He arrived there from Pendlebury, Manchester, in April 1867 and set about raising the cash for 'a new chapel, vestry and school-room' with 'the whole of the cost' – a total of £1400, apart from the organ – being paid on 28 November 1871. By then, however, his work in Dorset was done.

Rodgers claimed to have marshalled a thousand-stong band of emigrants, though only 80 arrived in Hawley, Clay County, Minnesota on 17 April 1873. They had sailed across the Atlantic from Liverpool on the steamship *City of Bristol*.

Most had been signed up at a meeting in Dorchester. The *Dorset County Chronicle* reported on 26 September 1872 that Revd Rodgers had already visited America to find a house for himself and his family:

'He was thoroughly delighted with what he had seen. There were millions of acres of fertile land only waiting to be tickled to make them smile a crop. Every farmer is his own landowner, every labourer his own master. The land was so cheap that a farm can be puschased for less than the rent of one of similar size in England for a year. He had arranged not only to take his wife and family there but he was also anxious to organise a colony – he had made arrangements with the Northern Pacific Railroad Company for the purpose.'

That was the problem. More might have followed, and New Yeovil appeared on the map, but hapless George Rodger had led his flock into a Hardyesque tragedy. His 'sober and industrious' band of 'good moral character' were settling on land in the Red River Valley that lay within 10 miles of the railway. Such ground, on either side of the track, was assumed to have been granted to the company and was therefore its to sell.

Unfortunately, the line happend to cross that of the St Paul and Pacific Railroad Company, at nearby Glyndon. As a result there were a total of 260,000 acres that were double-claimed by both companies. The dispute over the overlapping claims went to law and was settled in favour of the St Paul and Pacific line. Rodgers and his settlers were shocked to find that they had no title to land which had already been paid for, or obtained on credit, at ten shillings to £1-12s.-0d. an acre.

Disappointed settlers faced eviction and drifted across Clay County. They dispersed as far as the Badlands of South Dakota with a few then managing to return to England. Rodgers remained and died in Minnesota in December 1895. Muskoda dispensed with its Yeovil re-branding, and decayed into insignifance, though Hawley became the centre of a rich farming district. The original 'Pioneer Party' included Dorset names such as Fish, Luscombe, Raymond, Sawtell, and Vaughan.

STEEPLE

Lawrence quartering Washington

St Michael's Church – SY 912 809

As at Affpuddle, the arms of Lawrence quartering Washington are identical to the design on George Washington's signet ring. The first president of the United States of America was descended from this family.

Steeple is on the south side of the Purbeck Hills, west of Corfe Castle, on the other side of the great escarpment from the country house which became the Lawrence's Dorset seat, at Creech Grange.

The stars and stripes – correctly called bars and mullets, heraldically – joined the crusader cross of the Lawrence family when Edmund Lawrence married Agnes de Wessington, in 1390.

The coat of arms appears above the north door at Steeple Church, on a stone shield inside the south porch, and repeated several times inside the building, on the barrel-vaulted roof panels.

Heraldic bars and mullets which became the stars and stripes of the American flag (top right), and a standard of 1st Infantry Division which survived Omaha Beach, at St Michael's Church, Steeple.

Church of St Michael and All Angels at Steeple in the Isle of Purbeck.

Detail of the stars and stripes carving in the church porch at Steeple.

Flag of Washington, District of Columbia, hanging in Steeple Church.

THE DISTRICT OF COLUMBIA

WASHINGTON, D.C. 20004

July 25, 1977

WALTER E. WASHINGTON
Mayor

The Rector
Church of St. Michael
  & All Angels
Steeple, Dorset
England

Dear Rector:

We recently learned through Mr. George Honebon of Poole, that the Church of St. Michael & All Angels has an historic relationship with the family of George Washington, in whose honor our Nations Capital is named.

It was particularly interesting to see drawings of the stone armorial tablet depicting the Washington arms quartered with those of Lawrence. Because they are shown in our flag, the Washington arms are a very familiar sight in the District of Columbia.

Thinking that your parish might appreciate having some token of our mutual heritage, I have asked Mr. Honebon to carry with him on his return to England, this letter and the Flag of Washington, District of Columbia.

I know the citizens of our city join with me in this expression of friendship and best wishes to you and all the people of the community of Steeple, Dorset.

With warm personal regards.

                    Sincerely,

                    Walter E. Washington
                    Mayor
                    District of Columbia

Walter L. Washington, of Purbeck descent, wrote as mayor of the District of Columbia to Steeple's rector in 1977.

STUDLAND

USS *Constitution*

Old Harry Rocks – SZ 054 824

The USS *Constitution*, a heavily timbered single-deck frigate known as 'Old Ironsides', nearly became a wreck on the shingle beach between Ballard Point and Old Harry Rocks 'in the haze and mist of the night' on 17 January 1879. 'The boom of the guns quickly made known the fact,' as the warship announced her plight. She was homeward bound down the English Channel, from the Seine estuary in France, with products destined for the Paris Exhibition on the American side of the Atlantic.

Guns, chains, cable and other heavy items were removed to lighten the old three-masted sailing vessel in the morning. Five steamers then spent several hours trying to pull her clear. Eventually a Government tug arrived, from Southampton, and this additional assistance enabled them to release the *Constitution*. She was towed to Portsmouth, where only minor damage was found, and resumed her transatlantic voyage. Having survived this close encounter with the Dorset cliffs, *Constitution* was refurbished half a century later as an historic vessel, in Boston Navy Yard.

The frigate *Constitution* was one of three such warships ordered in 1794 and completed in 1797. They were constructed as a response to hostage-taking in the Mediterranean of 126 American sailors in Algiers, by the Muslim corsairs of the Barbary Coast, though at the time a ransom had to be paid to release them. The *Constitution* delivered revenge in 1804 as the American flagship for the bombardment of Tripoli by Commodore Edward Preble. Historically, many of the crew of the *Constitution* were British deserters and other mercenaries – enticed by high wages – and her crew of 419 seamen in 1807 included 149 British subjects and 29 other foreign nationals.

The most famous action of the USS *Constitution*, commanded by Captain Isaac Hull in the War of 1812 between Britain and the United States, was against HMS *Guerriere* which capitulated after two and half hours of combat on 19 August 1812. Her next victim, under Captain Bainbridge, was the frigate HMS *Java* which was reduced to a 'helpless hulk' during the British blockade of the east coast of the United States on 29 December 1813. The *Constitution* then had to put into Boston for repairs and did not return to sea until December 1814. Then, under Captain Charles Stewart, she captured the *Cyane* and *Levant* off the African coast on 20 February 1815. By this time, however, the peace treaty had been signed – several weeks earlier – though those at sea were unaware of the diplomatic developments.

STUDLAND

Exercise Smash

Fort Henry — SZ 038 828

Dorset's widest and sandiest seascape was chosen by Allied forces as the replica Normandy for live-firing invasion assaults in the months before D-Day. The lasting legacy of this activity, built by Canadian engineers in 1943, is Fort Henry which was named for their home base in Ontario. Overlooking Studland Bay, from scrub and sycamores on Redend Point, it is owned by the National Trust and extends along the seaward side of the grounds to the Manor House Hotel.

One of Britain's most important relics of the Second World War, it is over 90 feet long, with concrete walls almost 3-feet thick, above, in front, behind and below. Protected by these, with a narrow view as a horizonal slit provided with stepped recesses to reduce the chance of ricochets, and blast walls between each compartment, were a line of VIP field-glasses on an exceedingly noisy 18 April 1944. Users included King George VI, General Sir Bernard Montgomery, and General Dwight D. Eisenhower, the future President, as Supreme Commander Allied Forces Western Europe.

Fort Henry (centre), *built by Canadian Engineers in 1943, on Redend Point at Studland.*

Left and below: *Recessed slit for onlookers from the bomb-proof Fort Henry observation post on Redend Point.*

Exercise Smash landing on Studland beach, in rehearsals for D-Day, watched by King George VI on 18 April 1944.

'Big Red One' emblem of the United States 1st Infantry Division with Studland reflections.

Above, right and below: *United States Army half-track and troops in a re-enactment of Exercise Smash, at Studland, on 18 April 2002.*

Tarrant Rushton

Tarrant Rushton Aerodrome

Airmen's Corner — SY 950 061

Many Canadians and American soldiers and flyers had memories of Tarrant Rushton Aerodrome, which is now returned to agriculture and functioning as a great grain field, though the large hangars there still spell out its original purpose. The hardstanding of the more or less circular perimiter taxiway survives and is walkable as a public bridleway. There is a memorial beside the main entrance and its post-box at what has become known as Airmen's Corner on the road between Tarrant Rawston and Witchampton.

This airfield covered 2 square miles, with a series of hardened runways, and was in use from 1942, for airborne forces and secret cross-Channel flights by the Special Operations Executive, with spies and elite forces on missions behind enemy lines. As with any large aerodrome, it also attracted its share of Bomber Command and United States 8th Air Force 'strays', in need of a place to land.

A flak-damaged B-17 Flying Fortress of the United States Army Air Force limped back across the Channel on 5 January 1944 after sustaining 30 hits over Merignac airfield at Bordeaux.

The pilot proudly showed off his shell-shot bomber after he brought it down in a successful forced-landing at RAF Tarrant Rushton. He found himself among the gliders that were preparing for Exercise Nox. That was a major training programme that ran for the best part of a week.

Both specialities of airborne warfare were brought together on 20 January 1944, at RAF Tarrant Rushton, for Exercise Manitoba. It took its name from the participants. Firstly, eight Halifax aircraft of 298 Squadron carried the First Canadian Paratroop Brigade to a dropping-zone. Then ten Halifaxes, from the same Squadron, pulled Hamilcar gliders into the sky.

These were loaded with Tetrarch Mark VII light tanks which only just fitted into a glider. By 1944 considered too thinly armoured for normal tank warfare, this 7.5 ton vehicle had a two-pounder gun and a 7.92 mm Besa machine-gun, which were all that were considered necessary for taking on German tanks when it was made in 1939. In the scenario of an airborne landing, hopefully, it would be more likely to find itself in armoured reconnaissance or infantry support roles rather than facing the enhanced fire-power of frontline Panzers.

The gliders were released at 1000 feet. One Hamilcar overshot the landing area and ripped a Nissen hut apart as the tank shot forward from the debris. Both vehicle and driver survived.

Hundreds of wounded American soldiers were repatriated via Tarrant Rushton, in a fleet of Dakota transports, following the Battle of the Bulge — the German thrust into the snowy forests of the Ardennes — through Christmas in 1944. They were initially ferried to United States General Hospitals in the locality, at Blandford, Pamphill and St Leonards, and then dispersed to other centres for long term care or recuperation.

Dakota transport at RAF Tarrant Rushton.

Above and right: *Commemorating the 60th anniversary of D-Day, from a memorial beside a wartime hangar, at the entrance to former Tarrant Rushton Aerodrome in 2004.*

TOLPUDDLE

Tolpuddle Martyrs

Sycamore tree – SY 792 945

Known at the time as the Dorchester Labourers or the Dorset Unionists, five of the six Tolpuddle Martyrs who had been transported to Australia, went on to a new life in North America. In the late summer of 1833, following evening discussions under the sycamore tree on the village green, workers at Tolpuddle formed a Friendly Society of Agricultural Labourers. They then met in the upstairs of Thomas Standfield's cottage, to the east on the north side of the main road.

Both the Whig Government and supporters of the previous Tory adminstration united in resisting what they saw as the dangerous spread of northern trades unionism into the southern shire counties. Lord Melbourne, the Home Secretary, received warnings from Sir Robert Peel in London and magistrate James Frampton at Moreton House in the Dorset countryside. Charles Wollaston, visiting there during the agricultural riots of 1830, found it 'barricaded like an Irish mansion'.

In October 1833, Mr and Mrs Whetman who had a paint shop in Dorchester, were asked by James Loveless to prepare a banner with a 6-feet high representation of 'Death' and the words 'Remember Thine End'. They refused and the work was done elsewhere.

Local magistrates reacted in February 1834 by posting notices around Tolpuddle warning that 'mischieving and designing persons' were inducing labourers to 'enter into illegal societies or unions, to which they bind themselves by unlawful oaths'. Such activity rendered those involved 'guilty of felony and liable to be transported for seven years'.

At 6 am on 24 February 1834, George Loveless was arrested by a constable, while on his way to work in the fields. They proceeded to the homes of the others named in the indictment – George's younger brother, James Loveless; Thomas Standfield and his eldest son John Standfield; James Hammett; and James Brine. On 27 February 1834 the local newspaper, the *Dorset County Chronicle*, printed a Friendly Society oath of the sort that had been administered beneath the life-sized image of a skeleton, and followed it a week later with an editorial denouncing 'illegal combinations' as a matter of deep concern 'to all men of property, of whatever party'.

John Williams was appointed to the judiciary on 28 February 1834 and as Mr Baron Williams he conducted the Lent Assize in the Crown Court, Shire Hall, High West Street, Dorchester. The six Tolpuddle labourers appeared before him there on 15 March 1834. They were accused of administering a secret or unlawful oath contrary to the Mutiny Act, 1797. Mr Baron Williams ruled that the oath was unlawful despite its being accepted by the Crown that the men had not gathered together for a seditious purpose. Confirmation that it had been given, and that he was 'told to keep it secret' came from villager Edward Legg, who also said that the accused were 'all hard-working men' and that he had 'never heard a word against any of them'.

The men were found guilty but sentence was reserved. On 19 March 1834 the men were brought up from the cells, and Mr Baron Williams handed down the maximum punishment that was available to him, of seven years' transportation 'beyond the seas'. He accepted that the men were of previous good character but said that the sentence had a wider purpose:

'The object of all legal punishment is not altogether with the view of operating on the offenders themselves, but with a view to offering an example and warning.'

That night the windows in the vicarage at Tolpuddle were broken by stones. The transportations, to Australia, took place via Gosport and Plymouth. Agitation for their release spread to London, with petitions to Parliament and huge open-air demonstrations, which resulted in William IV giving the men a free pardon and the promise of passage back to England, signed by the King on 10 March 1836.

Eventually, as free-men once more, five of the six Tolpuddle Maryrs – excepting James Hammett – chose not to return to Dorset, with the ex-convicts and their families feeling the stigma of social ostracism and fearing that though no longer involved in active politics they would always be the first suspects if others started to arouse the community. Having travelled to the other side of the Earth and returned, they now looked in the opposite direction, towards an underpopulated region of the New World where they might feel free from intimidation.

British North America was the chosen destination. By the time they travelled, Liverpool and Cunard were replacing Bristol and Brunel, as the main transatlantic port and carrier. Whether they then proceeded via New York, or directly up the St Lawrence seaway, they arrived as Canadians welcomed 'an unprecedented influx of emigrants from Great Britain and Ireland, in a state of destitution, starvation and disease, unparalleled in the history of the province'.

The Tolpuddle refugees arrived in the mid-1840s. These were the Hungry Forties and many were sailing to escape the very distress against which the Dorchester Labourers had been protesting. The Loveless families were better provisioned and healthier than most but six-year-old Sina Loveless – youngest daughter of Betsy and George – died during the crossing and was buried at sea.

The destination was London in Ontario. Its 3000 population included a British garrison in the town, and the surrounding township comprised sparsely settled fields and woods dotted with remote farms and hamlets. From having been virtual serfs, earning a few shillings subsistence money a week, the Tolpuddle labourers became substantial landowners in terms of Dorset acreages.

George Loveless (1797–1874) acquired 100 acres at Bryanston from the 12th Concession, being half of Lot 11. He paid £25, in 1847, and took on a mortgage for the balance of the £150 price. Son Robert Loveless bought 100 acres of the 9th Concession, comprising the south half of Lot 10, in 1851. In 1856, George built a timber-framed house on 4th Concession ground at Fanshawe, Siloam, near London, Ontario. Betsy and George Loveless were buried in Siloam cemetery.

James Loveless (1808–73) and family initially moved to Bryanston. James was George Loveless's brother. James's daughter Emily was born to his second wife in 1853. By then he was sexton of North Street Methodist Church in London. James Loveless was buried in its cemetery but this was then sold for development and the body exhumed to Mount Plessant cemetery, London, Ontario.

James Brine (1812–1902) first bought a farm at Homesville, near Clinton, and then moved to Bayfield, also in Huron County. John Thomas Brine, born in 1845, was the first of the Tolpuddle offspring to be a native Canadian. He was followed by Louisiana, William, Evangeline, Charles, Elizabeth, Louise and Tillie. The family built a log cabin, Old Brine Homestead, in St Mary's, Blanshard Township, Perth County. Elizabeth and James Brine are buried in St Mary's cemetery, Blanshard.

John Standfield (1813–98), nephew of George and James Loveless, bought land from the 11th Concession, Lot 8, to the south of Bryanston in London township. He also acquired nearby Lot 10 on which he built Dorset Hall. The family was expanding, with the births of Wesley Loveless Standfield (1848), Herbert Thurgood Standfield (1850), Evangeline Standfield (1853) and Gertrude (1856). The enterprising John moved into London, establishing two stores, and later opened an hotel. He was appointed reeve of East London village and founded its choir. Elizabeth and John Standfield are buried in Mount Pleasant cemetery, London, Ontario.

Thomas Standfield (1790–1864) was either with, or living somewhere very close to his son's family, probably in one of their many properties. Diana and Thomas

Standfield are buried in Siloam cemetery, near London, in the plot beside that of Betsy and George Loveless.

They experienced entirely different circumstances from those in England. Henceforth the efforts and rewards of existence resulted from personal labour rather than being carried out as third-party endeavours on behalf of feudal masters. The Tolpuddle families went back in time to a Methodist society in the mould of its original Wesleyan founders. This was authoritarian – with democracy being regarded as much an anathama as sin

– and was already under threat in England from the new philosophy of free-thought. They left their politics in England and the Tolpuddle connection remained a well-kept secret for most of their time in Canada.

The Tolpuddle Martyrs' Memorial Cottages at Tolpuddle, erected by the Trades Union Congress in 1934, overlook a wide roadside lawn. A Portland stone frieze by Liverpool sculptor Thomas Dagnall is entitled 'The Tolpuddle Six'. It depicts a despairing George Loveless beside five featureless blocks of limestone.

Above: *Props supporting the historic sycamore tree, on the green at Tolpuddle, below which its agricultural workers met in 1834.*

Right: *Remaining original buildings at Botany Bay Barn, seen in 1979, where prisoners en route from Dorchester to the hulks in Portsmouth and transportation to Australia spent their last night in Dorset.*

Headstone to James Hammett, unveiled by George Lansbury on 31 August 1934, commemorating the centenary of the only Tolpuddle Martyr to return home.

Above: *James Hammett's grave lies in the shadow of lime trees and the tower of the parish church at Tolpuddle.*

Right: *George Loveless, sculpted by Thomas Dagnall, in front of the Memorial Cottages at Tolpuddle.*

WAREHAM

Warburton Pike

Furzebrook House – SY 932 837

Warburton Mayer Pike (1861–1915) was used to being alone, as his mother died when he was five, and his father when he was eight. The son of Wareham and Furzebrook clayfield owner John William Pike (1814–69), he began his expeditions into the Purbeck Hills from Furzebrook House. The ball clay workings in what is now the Blue Pool were at the hub of a miniature tramway system which linked mines and drying and mixing sheds with a wharf at Ridge on the tidal stretch of the River Frome. Beyond the industrial zone rose the 634-feet cone shaped summit of Creech Barrow Hill, and a heathland wilderness teeming with lizards and snakes.

The six Pike siblings each inherited a small fortune on reaching the age of maturity which was then twenty-one-years-old. Elder brother Marmaduke Pike was said to have led Warburton astray, causing him to drop out of Oxford and become a West End playboy, with the result that he contracted syphilis which affected both health and behaviour for the rest of his relatively short life.

Warburton's boyhood enthusiam for railways, steamboats and natural history was transferred on to a broader canvas when he decided to emigrate to Canada. He again headed for the hills and crossed the continent to British Columbia from where he ventured into the Yukon and the Arctic. Financial interests in the newly built Cassiar Central Railway and gold panning operations near Dease Lake enabled him to buy his own estate, on Saturna Island, where the highest hill is named Mount Warburton in his memory. St Mary Magdalene Church, on Mayne Island, stands on land he donated to the community.

Warburton Pike was the North American equivalent of a big game hunter, describing his expeditions and experiences in *The Barren Ground of Northern Canada*, in 1892, and *Through the Subarctic Forest* in 1896. By now he was generally known as 'Crazy Pike' as his entreprenureal skills stretched to breaking point and he fell further into debt. As his mental condition deteriorated he felt forced to return to England.

There he received some recognition from his peers, in the form of membership of the prestigious Royal Geographical Society, but continued to suffer seriously from depression which caused his admission to a sanatorium in Bournemouth. World events would hardly have helped, in the second year of the First World War, when he killed himself with a pen-knife.

WEYMOUTH

Clark and Endecott Memorial

Alexandra Gardens – SY 681 788

A seafront memorial in Alexandra Gardens, opposite the Pier Pavilion, commemorates Richard Clark and John Endecott. Clark was the 'Captain and pilot of Weymouth who in 1583 sailed thence to join Sir Humphrey Gilbert's voyage of discovery to Newfoundland', playing a role in establishing the first British colony in North America at St John's, Newfoundland.

John Endecott (1589–1665), who was born in Chagford, Devon, and grew up in Dorchester, became another Weymouth adventurer. With five others, he bought from the Plymouth Council in England the reputed title to a strip of North America that was 60 miles wide and 'extended from sea to shining sea', from the Atlantic to the Pacific. This included Salem and Massachusetts, where he sailed in the *Abigail* on 19 March 1628. There were 20 or 30 in the party and they made their landfall at Naumkeag on 6 September 1628. The settlers renamed it Salem.

On his arrival, Endecott became the first Governor of 'the Company of Massachusetts Bay in New England' and retained the post, with only a few breaks, until his death. Described as 'a stout soldier' and a 'Puritan of Puritans', Endecott sought to establish the 'City of God' in the New World. He had a reputation for taking direct action, such as cutting down a maypole on which satirical anti-Puritan handbills had been posted. In 1634 he became enraged at the sight of the red cross of St George being carried by a Salem bandsman. He denounced the flag as an 'idolatrous Popish emblem' and cut out the cross from the banner in a public protest.

To the south, Virginia was devoutly Anglican, and the Dutch held sway on the Hudson River. This left the 'stern and rockbound coast' where the Pilgrim Fathers had landed. The flow of immigrants became a flood,

with 1000 arriving in the first six months of 1630, and upwards of 10,000 in 1634.

There was considerable disharmony among existing migrants when they heard that Endecott and his fellow patentees had purchased the 'property and privileges' of the Dorchester Company at Naumkeag and Cape Ann. They opposed the cultivation of tobacco as 'injurious to both health and morals' and banned the use of the Book of Common Prayer. Dissolute members of the community at Mount Wollaston – named for Wollaston in Dorchester but now renamed Quincy – were brought under control. Endecott visited Mount Wollaston (popularly known as Mount Merry) to rebuke the inhabitants 'for their profanity, and admonished them to look to it that they walked better'. John Endecott, described as a 'stout soldier' became Governor of the 'Company of the Massachusetts Bay in New England'.

The rights that 'Zion's Saviour' proclaimed for himself and fellow puritans were denied to Quakers whom he accused of 'open capital blasphemies'. The last years of his life were marked and marred by correspondence across the water with King Charles II and his Secretary, Sir William Morrice. They hoped that Endecott would be replaced 'at the next election' by 'any other person of good reputation'. By then, however, Endecott had died. He was buried in the 'Chapel burying-ground' at Boston but his memorial there is said to have been destroyed by British redcoats during the American Revolutionary War.

The memorial in Weymouth was unveiled in 1914 by Endecott's direct descendant, the former Miss Mary Crowinshield Endicott, from New England. The fifth generation of the family had changed the second syllable of their name from 'e' to 'i', Mary Endicott was the third and final wife of Joseph Chamberlain

(1836–1914) who had been Colonial Secretary from 1895 until 1902 when he became the first such British minister to made an official visit to an overseas colony. This was South Africa, but the fact-finding mission precipitated his resignation, because the Cabinet rejected his attempt to extend preferential tariff rates to imports of colonial food.

Mary Endicott 'made life once more a gloroius and a hopeful thing' by marrying Joseph Chamberlain in 1888. In the process she created another transatlantic link as the stepmother to future Prime Minister Neville Chamberlain (1869–1940) who took Britain into the Second World War on 3 September 1939.

Above: *Timeless scene as a fishing boat enters Weymouth Harbour.*

Right: *The memorial in Alexandra Gardens to mariners Richard Clark and John Endecott.*

WEYMOUTH

Joseph Bucklin

Causeway House, Radipole – SY 661 814

Joseph Bucklin fired the first shot in the American Revolution. He traced his settler origins to William Bucklin (born 1609), or Buckman, who came from the River Wey in Dorset and emigrated with the Winthrop Fleet in 1630. He has been linked to Causeway House, Radipole, at Weymouth, and the family name still attaches to the local landscape. A mile to the west are South Buckland and Buckland Ripers hamlet.

Bucklin lived on Rhode Island for most of his life. His moment in history came at Lexington on the night of 18-19 April 1775 when Major John Pitcairn and his British redcoats from Boston marched into the village, en route to Concord where a congress under the presidency of John Hancock had declared the virtual independence of the Province of Massachusetts Bay in defiance of the Governor, General Thomas Gage. Pitcairn's men were attempting to confiscate Patriot munitions.

The column was ambushed at Lexington, by colonial minute-men, from behind a stone wall. In the words of essayist and poet Ralph Waldo Emerson, 'the embattled farmers stood, and fired the shot heard round the world'. Bucklin's shot was joined by a volley of fire and a total of eight redcoats lay dead on the grass of the village common. Nearly fourteen months were to elapse before reaction and rebellion evolved into the Declaration of Independence.

D-Day Memorial

The Esplanade – SY 680 793

Weymouth's other American memorial, on the Esplanade opposite the Royal Hotel, commemorates the sailing from Weymouth and Portland of the American assault force – including the 1st Infantry Division and Ranger units – that saw the bloodiest D-Day fighting with more than 3000 casualties on Omaha Beach in Normandy. The plaque records that 517,816 troops and 144,093 vehicles were embarked through Weymouth and Portland by the 14th Major Port, United States Army, between the 6 June 1944 and the end of the war on 7 May 1945.

Dorset was the Concentration Area for the marshalling of men and matèriel for V Corps of the United States Army (Force O for Omaha). This comprised the 1st United States Infantry Division, the 2nd United States Infantry Divison, the 2nd United States Armored Division, and two Ranger Battalions. More than 80,000 American soldiers occupied Dorset. BUKO (West) was the Build Up Control Organisation for the First United States Army and the Second British Army, with headquarters at Portsmouth, and came under the control of Brigadier Duke, who retired as Major-General Sir Gerald Duke (1910–92). BUKO (East) was a bogus logistical operation set up in Dover to deceive the Germans into thinking the attack would come in the Calais area.

H-Hour for Dorset's Americans, the hour they were to begin the assault on Omaha Beach, was re-set to 06.45 hours on 6 June 1944, after having been delayed for 24 hours by windy weather. In the event, the troops first touched down on the sands of Normandy at 06.34, but that was all that went ahead of schedule for V Corps.

They attacked on a broad front – 10 miles wide – with two regimental combat teams. One each was from the 29th Infantry Division and the 1st Infantry Division, supplemented by Ranger Battalions. The 29th Division was tasked to capture Vierville-sur-mer as its initial target, while the 1st Division was to secure Colleville-sur-mer about 3 miles to the east. The landing beaches for Force O extended from Point du Hoc to Colleville, to the north-west of Bayeux which is famous for an invasion tapestry depicting a Norman assault in the other direction, beginning at Pevensey on 28 September 1066.

Heavy seas and numerous underwater obstacles caused considerable losses to the leading wave of Americans in amphibious tanks and landing craft. Aerial bombing had been hampered by poor visibility, and many bombs fell some distance inland, added to which the Naval bombardment was also largely ineffective due to the topography of the ground.

Worse was to follow. German coastal forces had been recently augmented by the 352nd Infantry Division, a field formation which happened to be holding a stand-to exercise, and was manning the defences as the Americans came ashore. They ran into an enemy division that was ready for action and were pinned to the beaches. Likewise the Ranger Battalions on the right flank were met with stiff resistance and V Corps received the bloodiest reception of all the D-Day landings.

For several hours it had seemed that they might well be thrown back into the sea. Extreme sacrifice and gallantry – leaving a thousand dead and twice that injured – had by nightfall achieved a beachhead, a mile in depth, between Vierville and Colleville. This foothold was established after follow-up regimental teams arrived. These reinforcements enabled the storming of the enemy batteries. Forward elements moved 2 miles inland, pushing for higher ground, in the vicinity of Formigny.

The novelist Ernest Hemingway arrived as a war correspondent with the assault forces, aboard the troopship *Dorothea L. Dix*, from Portland.

Major Stanley Bach, the liaison officer giving General Cota's orders to 1st Infantry Division assault troops on the beach, scrawled these potted descriptions of the day on a couple of old envelopes which were his only available paper:

'*11.30. Mortar, rifle, 88mm and machine gun fire so heavy on beach, it's either get to ridge in back of beach or be killed.*

'*Noon. Beach high tide, bodies floating. Many dead Americans on beach at high-water mark.*

'*12.15. Heavy mortar and 88mm fire started on beach from east end to west end – series of five shells in spots. Direct hit on Sherman tank, men out like rats – those still alive.*

'*12.30 LCT (Landing Craft Tanks) hit two mines, came on in – hit a third, disintegrated and rear end sank. At burst of shell two Navy men went flying through the air into the water and never came up.*

'*14.40. More mortar fire and more men hit. LCVP (Landing Craft Vital Personnel) unload five loads of men, they lie down on beach, five get killed by mortar fire, the rest run up to fox holes we left a couple of hours ago.*

'*16.50. Established CP (Command Post) and saw first time the 1st Division friends who were quiet, fighting men – gave me heart.*

'*17.00. Prisoners began to come up the road – a sorry looking bunch in comparison to our well-fed and equipped men.*

'*Dusk. I've seen movies, assault training demonstrations and actual battle but nothing can approach the scenes on the beach from 11.30 to 14.00 hours – men being killed like flies from unseen gun positions. Navy can't hit 'em, air cover can't see 'em, so Infantry had to dig 'em out.*'

The Americans could indeed have lost the beach if the German High Command had not held back their reserve units, thinking that the Normandy assaults were a feint and that the main invasion force would land between the Seine and Calais. Overlord fielded a total of 39 divisions but the Germans wildly exaggerated its strength, believing that between 75 and 85 divisions had been assembled for the Allied Second Front; this belief caused them to hold back their forces in preparation for the non-existent second half.

Left: *D-Day memorial, unveiled in 1947, on the Esplanade opposite the Royal Hotel.*

Below: *Local child climbs on to a GI Jeep (background right) as military policeman Dan Ewton poses for the camera at Weymouth in April 1944.*

The elite 2nd Ranger Battalion of the United States Army marching to war, along the Esplanade at Weymouth on 4 June 1944, with Lieutenant Bob Eldin (right) running to catch up with Major James Earl Rudder (foreground).

American assault troops 'doing the Lambeth walk' on Custom House Quay, Weymouth, in mock exhilaration on 4 June 1944.

Assault landing craft beside Weymouth Quay and the landing stage station (right), being loaded with stores on 3 June 1944.

The view from the shore as Negro 'Static Troops' passed down boxes of 'C&K' rations into landing craft moored beside the steps to the west of the railway station on Weymouth Quay, 3 June 1944.

American Rangers being packed like sardines into assault landing craft beside Weymouth Quay on 4 June 1944.

Above: *GIs singing, prior to being loaded on USS* Henrico *in Weymouth Harbour, on 4 June 1944.*

Left above: *United States landing craft and barrage balloons between Devonshire Buildings and the Pavilion Theatre, Weymouth Quay, on 4 June 1944.*

Left: *Anti-aircraft gunners, Stewards Mates Jones and Furrell Browning from Dallas, keeping watch for the Luftwaffe from USS* Henrico *in Weymouth Harbour on 5 June 1944.*

Weymouth cinema usherette Doris Mockridge married Private Ernest Webster of the United States 1st Infantry Division – the figure '1' on his shoulder shield – but by the time of the GI wedding he had lost a leg on Omaha Beach.

Omaha Beach and its vast American war cemetery (centre top) seen from a Dakota, on a 50th anniversary flight over the invasion beaches, in 1994.

Above and left: Veteran wartime Dakota G-AMPZ heading towards Omaha Beach on a commemorative flight in 1994.

WHITCHURCH CANONICORUM

Sir George Somers

Berne Farm – SY 388 944

Sir George Somers (1554–1610) was a veteran of three voyages to the Azores and an attack on the Spanish fleet. He was knighted in 1603 and settled down to a quieter life at Berne Farm, Whitchurch Canonicorum, which he had bought in 1587.

He represented Lyme Regis in Parliament and in 1605 was its mayor. By 1606, however, he was playing an active part, as a 'man of good skill in all passages' in planning the colonisation of Virginia. In 1609, the old salt had a fleet of nine vessels under his command and was sailing in the *Sea Venture*, to relieve Jamestown. The colony was in a state of siege and starvation as a result of Indian hostilities.

After eight weeks at sea the boats were scattered by a hurricane and on 25 July 1608 the *Sea Venture* was wrecked on the rocks of an unoccupied group of mid-atlantic islands. These had been sighted by Juan Bermudas, a Spaniard in 1515. At that time, however, Bermuda was known as the Isle of Devils.

Somers took possession in the name of the King, James I, and indeed they are still a Crown colony. For Somers and his crew they were a lifesaver, providing 'sufficient of many kinds of fishes with hooks, so plentiful thereof that a man step into the water, they will come round about him, so that he was fane to get out for fear of biting.' Fowl 'in great number' provided eggs, and there were also turtles, young birds and edible berries. There was enough timber for shipbuilding though it was not until ten months later that the *Patience* and *Deliverance* were ready to continue the journey to the American continent.

They arrived at Jamestown on 23 May 1610. A second relief force came from England and Somers decided to return to Bermuda, where he was to die from a 'surfeit of eating a pig'. His son Matthew had George's heart buried on St George's island and the body was embalmed for the return journey to England and Whitchurch Canonicorum. As for the islands, these were first known as Virginiola but Somers' Islands followed until the inevitable corruption Summer Islands combined their founder's name and the climatic conditions. Ultimately the original name of Bermuda prevailed.

Back at home, via sailor Sylvester Jourdain who lived above Whitchurch at Fishpond and accompanied Somers on the voyage, the story reached Shakespeare and became the setting for *The Tempest*. Berne Farm is midway along the lane between Whitchurch Canonicorum and Charmouth but lost its rustic looks and high thatched roof when it caught fire on being struck by lightning in 1926.

There is a high brass plate to Sir George Somers in Whitchurch Canonicorum parish church, put there in 1908, on the south wall of the chancel. His body is beneath the floor of the vestry and has a latin epitaph which is delightful in translation: 'Alas Virginia's summer so soon passed but promising an English spring of happy rain and flowers ...'

The countryside of Whitchurch Canonicorum, in the Marshwood Vale, was home to the mariner who founded Bermuda and the writer who recorded the momentous shipwreck.

Berne Farm, between Whitchurch Canonicorum and Charmouth, was the birthplace of Sir George Somers in 1554.

The mariner Sir George Somers left Whitchurch Canonicorum, in 1610, on a voyage which resulted in the colonisation of Bermuda.

Tempest Cottage, the home of mariner Silvester Jourdain who sailed with Somers to Bermuda and brought home to England the shipwreck story that William Shakespeare turned into a play.

The direct link between Dorset and Bermuda was re-established by Sir Alan Cobham from Tarrant Rushton (centre right), *and pilot Donald 'Pathfinder' Bennett* (left) *with a non-stop flight-refuelled Lancastrian which crossed the Atlantic in 1947.*

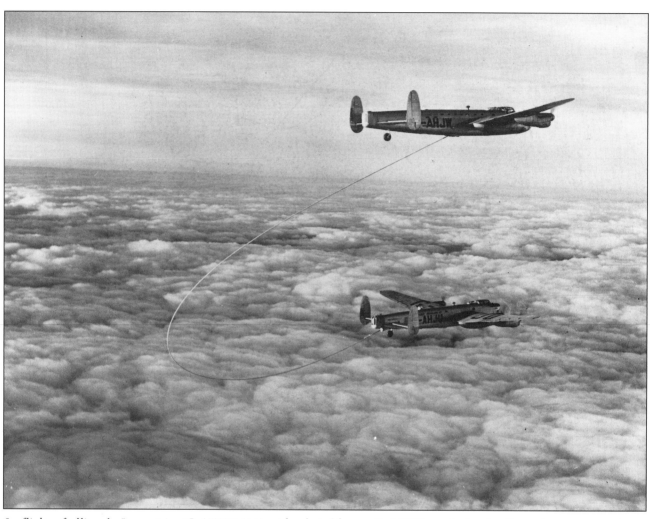

In-flight refuelling, by Lancastrian G-AHJW (top) with a looped hose to G-AHJU, on the London-Bermuda non-stop service.